Publisher:
TTG
Bloom Blueprint Books

Editor :
Meritokpes

Photo Credit for Olivia | Precious & Naomi
Chandler Hatch Photography

Visit www.Thebreakthroughblueprints.com

Table of Contents

THE ARCHITECTS ANNOUNCEMENT

Khalilah Olokunola

Spiritual Gift: *Apostolic*

Wife , Mom , Servant Leader

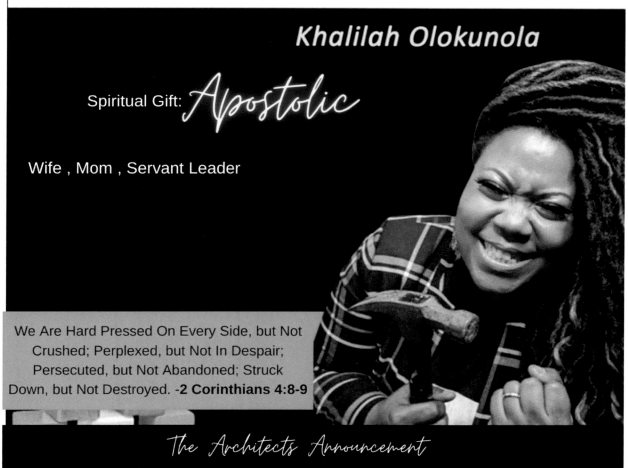

We Are Hard Pressed On Every Side, but Not Crushed; Perplexed, but Not In Despair; Persecuted, but Not Abandoned; Struck Down, but Not Destroyed. **-2 Corinthians 4:8-9**

The Architects Announcement

I don't know anyone that believes it's easy to share a part of you that you hid, a part of you that you worked hard to keep covered because of the shame & the pain that comes with it.

I know it wasn't easy for me . I carried the burden that came with my testimony for so long . The burden of :

Being assaulted by family members and family friends who wanted to play house
That unhinged me

Spending more than 4 years in prison
That halted me

Living more than 10 years confused about my identity and ability to survive
That hindered me

Being homeless & hopeless
 That hurt me

Having kids at an early age
That helped me

We all have testimonies that we carry , conceal but rarely communicate about . It was at a pivotal point in my life where opening up my mouth propelled me into my mandate .
There is SO MUCH more to what God has done in my life and what He is going to do in yours but like Ecclesiastes says there is a season for every activity under the sun and I am a firm believer that God has an appointed time set aside in His plan for you to testify.
- It's a time when it's needed
- It's a time when someone has been praying and fervently seeking Him for answers and an assignment
- It's a time when He wants to take trauma from a tragedy and birth tenacity in you
- It's a time where you are ready to rise as the remnant and become who you have been called to be.
- Nothing is by accident in the Kingdom ….
- Nothing could have prepared me for purpose like life did.
- It was the pain that tried to paralyze me but instead pushed me
- It was the failure that forced me to find my fight.
- It was rejection that reminded me of my source of strength
- It was God who used my shortcomings to strategically birth the builder in me so that I can birth it in other people.

My heart is that these Breakthrough Blueprint chapters from these powerful women will inspire | incite & ignite something in you to use your testimony as a tool .

PKO

Chapter 2

Courageously Commissioned

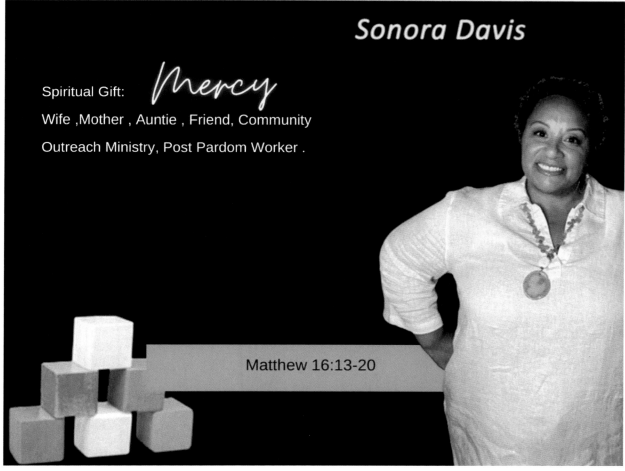

Sonora Davis

Spiritual Gift: *Mercy*

Wife ,Mother , Auntie , Friend, Community Outreach Ministry, Post Pardom Worker .

Matthew 16:13-20

I am filled with much gratitude for this life altering opportunity that was created in the Makers space by Pastor Khalilah Olokunola. This has been challenging and rewarding. This redesigning process created exchanges through connection, conversation and confession enabling me to see me, and the Christ working in me. Allowing me to rediscover my calling, my God given assignment utilizing His gifts and the pain of some life experiences, purposed for my promise.

My name is Sonora Davis. I am a Wife, Mother, Sister, Auntie, Friend, Outreach Ministry Coordinator and Community birth worker. I am committed and called to action, knowing that whatever I go through is never just for me. It is to be used as a tool to elevate the framework of my house that has been placed on a solid foundation in Christ, a house to bless and build the kingdom of God.

For as long as I can remember, I have always had great empathy for others and their trials and sufferings. When Mercy was revealed to be at the top of my list there was no surprise. I feel others pain deeply which moves me to provide an open door to demonstrate the gift of counsel within me, allowing one to lay their burdens down. The ability to create safe and sacred spaces are of absolute importance to me. The spiritual gift of mercy is something that God gives to us to give to others. The richness of God's mercy is truly a spiritual gift that brings us salvation through his Son, Jesus Christ.
I am commanded to give what I don't deserve to receive. His mercies are new everyday. The lord has given me the courage to trust him through my trials. I intimately know him as Father, Son and Holy Spirit. The lover of my soul has commissioned me to be used as his hands and feet to help the afflicted in spirit. To lift up the arms of those who have lost their fight.

As I approach my ring of fire. I take a moment to gaze at its glory and many dimensions attached to it. The brilliance of its light captures my soul. As I inhale the heat's ignition, I find the fortitude to release my fears. I am motivated and persuaded to push. In this moment, I realize the benefit of the burn through the stretching of my faith. I am a living miracle, I receive the crowning of a rebirth turning the pain into my purpose and promise. I am Courageously Commissioned.

I thoroughly enjoy serving my community through planned events that bring families together of all races and ages . Especially those in areas of neglect and isolation. My heart is mamas and babies. I've been called to empower the young mother who feels abandoned, lost and forgotten. A young mother who is isolated without the insulation of a mother or sister in Christ, she has no one to hold her close to the Father. No one to intercede, leaving her and her children vulnerable to the world and its systems. No one to show her how to become a curse breaker making cycles stop with her. Securing her faith and legacy in the one who holds it all in his hands. In this season it is time to pass down blessings and not curses! To provide safe places of refuge for families regardless of what their hell looks like, where they can feel loved and nurtured. I have been called to speak life to her dead areas, resuscitating her will to fight in such perilous times.

Courageously Commissioned

Confess

Peter's preparation of discipleship would lead him to his proclamation of faith. The question of the identity of Jesus as the Christ, the Son of the living God. Peter's confession of faith was so strong that now Jesus could share with his disciples the blueprint of the church and its everlasting power. "And the gates of hell shall not prevail against it". This good news of the Gospel gets me fired up. His word lets me know that as a believer in Christ and inspired by the Spirit. We are commissioned to engage in warfare and we will be victorious! Jesus gives Peter the keys to the kingdom directly tied to our salvation. We all have the keys of the kingdom because we can proclaim entrance into the kingdom through Christ and the work of redemption. Christ builds his church on a statement of faith with the expectation of a fight!

One of my favorite movies is Gi Jane, mostly because when Lieutenant O'Neil set her mind on becoming a Navy Seal nothing could stop or break her. The more she was attacked the harder she pursued her goal. What if you pursued Jesus with an expectation of a fight. Can you see yourself a saint and a soldier on the battlefield of His grace and mercy. I believe we were born again and born to fight approaching the gates with the keys in our hands, worshiper and warrior.

These last 6 months have proven that we as a nation have been in the fight of our lives. If you are reading this, you are still in the number redeemed and recruited! I pray you believe that the fight has been fixed. We are hard pressed on every side, but not crushed; perplexed,but not in despair; persecuted, but not abandoned, struck down, but not destroyed. 2Corinthians4:8,9. I am encouraged that your faith may be renewed and strengthened. As you continue to fight my sister put on the whole armor of God. Watching and praying for we are righteous and radical on the battlefield of the Lord.

I know what it is like to have faith in times of fear of what the future will hold. On my journey with the Lord I can say that I have encountered some things! I Thank you.I was covered and kept in the palm of your sovereign hand, dangers seen and unseen. A little girl abandoned by her father and afraid of what the future would be like without him. I was neglected, molested by those assigned to protect and nurture. At the age of eleven the Lord would capture my heart. He replaced anger with the love of my heavenly father calling me his own. I would trade abandonment for assurance. With every turn and obstacle in the face of my fear you have always given me an opportunity to grow my faith in you. For you are always establishing your grace and mercy for which I could never repay. Before my total surrender to you our relationship was one of you pursuing me right in the middle of my mess. I am so grateful that even now your pursuit of me is un-mitigating.

When I looked for love in all the wrong places you were there. Lord you were there when I made choices contrary to will and your way you were there!
As I look for self worth and acceptance in everything but you… Your consistent love pulled me out taking me from afflicted to anchored in you. Even in my darkest hours. A mother of three daughters 9, 3 and 5months old divorced and depleted. You held me close, sending me mamas and sisters who intentionally created safe spaces to love on me and my girls. As you held me, I held my daughters even closer clinging to your word holding it close to my heart. Psalm 16:5 NLT Lord, you alone are my inheritance, my cup of blessing . You guard all that is mine.

Courageously Commissioned

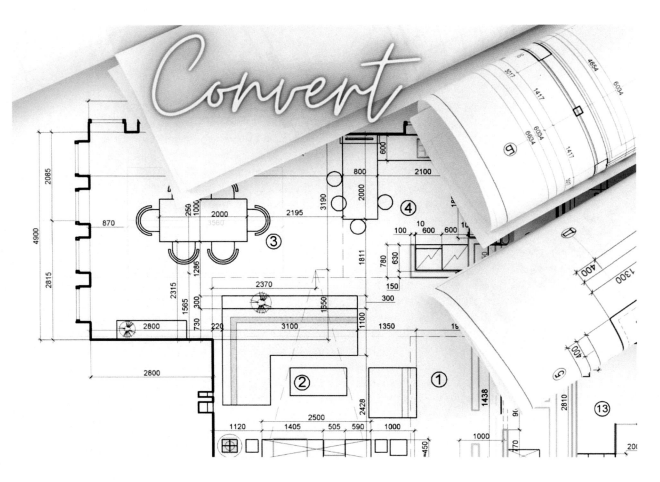

After 3 years Lord you would anoint me a curse breaker! Father God you already knew that my mother was the same age I was with three children the exact age as my daughters when she divorced my father. In 3 years you would send me my husband breaking the curse of single motherhood. You have blessed beyond measure Lord, you sent me my beloved great heart Brian Davisloving me and my girls, as he loves you. Father God you took me from guarded to abundantly grateful.

Praise God, my husband Brian Davis I would marry in April of 2009. The task of blending a family of 10 children 5 boys 5 girls 3 children of which were in college. 3 sets of natural siblings and 2 additional. My husband was a single father of 7 children 5 of which were adopted. The task of blending a family of this size and magnitude was daunting to say the least. Tested and tried by fire, kept by his grace and mercy. Five months later I would lose my favorite cousin. Suddenly, I watched her suffering in her last days by her side, tearing me apart. The grief of her loss was unbearable. She left us way too soon, it could have been me Lord. Covered by your love you comforted my sorrows.

From Pain to Purpose

Through my pain Lord you have equipped me with gifts to be used by you
To encourage and empower. Lord your preparation of me will make succession for the proclamation of faith working in your power according to my purpose and promise!

Courageously Commissioned

If you're reading this declare this out loud

7 I AM's

Today I am an instrument of my faith to be used by God. For his glory!

Today I am a devoted nurturer sustained by God's mercy and grace!

Today I am redeemed and recruited in the army God by the blood of Jesus!

Today I am forgiven and healed from my yesterdays, peace and promise is my portion!

Today I am commissioned to grow making impactful contributions in my life and the life of others!

Today I am confident and courageously qualified through my redeemer to be a mediator to those who are suffering insearch of a savior!

Coouragously Commissioned

Lord I come to you as humbly as I know how. To thank you. For your everlasting love. I thank you for being a mind regulator, my thoughts are connected to heaven, my heart overflowing with gratitude. I am compelled and inspired to action for your glory.

Lord I know where gratitude resides fear and negativity can not exist. Lord I thank you for in you there is no lack your supply endless peace and provision is my portion.

I put all in your hands Jesus, use me as your vessel. I thank you for my health, love, abilities, family, friends, and most of all this life and the will to fight for your gospel. I will do great things in the name of Jesus I pray.

Courageously Commissioned

Chapter 3

Reigning in Royalty

Precious Bernard

Spiritual Gift: *Administration*

Child of God, a wife, a mother, a daughter, a friend, a minister of the gospel, and a lover of people and music.

1 Peter 2:9

But you are a chosen people, a royal priesthood, a holy nation, God's special possession, that you may declare the praises of him who called you out of darkness into his wonderful light.

Grace and peace to you! I am so grateful that you have taken the time to share in this opportunity with myself and all of the other phenomenal women who have shared their story. My name is Precious Bernard. I am a child of God, a wife, a mother, a daughter, a friend, a minister of the gospel, and a lover of people and music. My most dominant gift is that of Administration. As an administrator, I am an organizer. I lend my time and talents to share steps with people and organizations in order to help them accomplish what they set out to accomplish. We all need someone on our side. Someone that will help guide us along our way.

We were created for relationship and thrive whenever we use our connections the right way. For instance, before a high school student graduates, he or she must talk to a guidance counselor. This counselor observes/listens to the heart and interests of those assigned to them. In turn, they use their knowledge, training, and experience to outline the most beneficial path to help get the student to their desired destination.

The purpose of this chapter is not for me to outline your life, but to encourage you to open up your heart to your Creator and give Him the most intimate details of your life.

He knows us better than we know ourselves, so why not seek Him to figure out His plans for your life. We were created for His glory and to be in relationship with Him. He longs to affirm who you are and what He has called you to be. Allow God to be your guide and help you accomplish all of the wonderful plans that He has for you. Whether you realize it or not, you are an heir of the most High God and his choicest blessings await you. You have been called to Reign in Royalty, and this is the purpose of this chapter.

My life has been filled with seasons where I did not recognize who I was. I did not recognize my value, nor did I understand my worth. As a result, I was vulnerable and allowed myself to be used in areas that should have remained sacred in my life. Even still, God with his amazing self has a way that's mighty sweet of finding His way to your heart. He captured my heart and reminded me that I belong to Him and that He loves me with an everlasting love. I now know beyond the shadow of a doubt that I am the apple of His eye and that I am worthy to receive His love. I feel that my experiences have opened the door for me to relate to every young woman that He places in my path. When we come out of a situation, it is our responsibility to encourage and build someone with the same encouragement that we received (1 Thessalonians 5:11). Like the guidance counselor, I am called to listen to His precious children, share His love, build them up with the Word of the Lord, and encourage them with the testimonies of my experience. Our experiences may not be the exact same, but I have learned that the underlying principle in our strategy for success is the same.

Reigning in Royalty

Always remember that God has called you to Reign in Royalty; He has given YOU dominion to rule over every situation. Your ability to reign in royalty lies in your ability to open up your heart to receive God's love for you, walk in the promises/authority that He has offered you, and when you come out, reach back and pull up your fellow man. If you have ever felt vulnerable, felt as if you were not good enough, settled for less than in life, or have ever felt that you were unworthy to be loved, then this chapter is for you. The Bible says that we overcome by the blood of the Lamb and by the word of our testimonies (Revelation 12:11).

God has given me a newfound confidence and I would love to share my story with you.

One of the greatest lessons we can learn in life is to recognize that there are people that God places in our life that often times have gone the very path that we may have to take. The more time you spend with these people, experience, wisdom, and sound advice is bound to be revealed. Our response to what is shared, in return, can be one of two things: either we take heed to what they are sharing and avoid the countless headaches and heart aches of traveling down the path they travelled; or we can completely disregard their advice and experience the situation for ourselves. The latter often results in some type of self-destruction, and this is certainly not God's will for our life.

I honestly believe that it is God's desire for us to have a life full of Godfidence (confidence in Him) and peace (assurance, knowing wholeheartedly that He has your best interest at heart).

I believe that when He places experience and wisdom before us, this is divine guidance at its finest; and, He is such a gentleman that He will not force us to follow the straight and narrow path that has been placed before us. Proverbs 19:20 (ESV) says it best, "Listen to advice and accept instruction, that you may gain wisdom in the future."

Reigning in Royalty

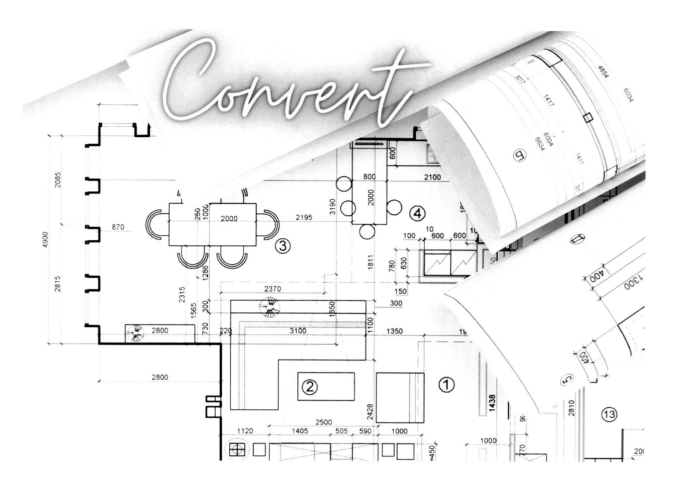

Nothing God does is by happenstance, and as we know, He will allow everything that happens to work for our good (Romans 8:28). As a matter of fact, I am absolutely certain that He is allowing me to share my story with you is for a reason. That reason is simply to be encouraged and to overcome! There was a time that I was utterly embarrassed about my story, and figured that everyone would think different of me if I even told the minutest detail of my story. However, the very first time I felt the inkling to share my story, it was like preparing to freefall off of a cliff. Either I was going to jump by opening up my mouth and allowing God to use the words that He gave me to comfort the person standing before me, or I was going to stand still and my efforts would cause me to be fall once again as a victim of my past.

When I shared my story, the young lady confirmed that it was meant for me to share my story because she was going through a similar situation. All I could say in my head was, "You never really know what someone is going through!"

I almost allowed the fear that Satan tried to implant in my mind to stop me from ministering to my sister in need. The enemy's intention is to kill, steal, and destroy; but Jesus has come that we may have life of abundance (John 10:10).

We serve a God that is willing to intercede on your behalf. He will fight for you, just so that you can have an abundance of love, joy, hope, and peace.

If you are reading this, I'd ask that you take a moment and clear your mind. Literally, close your eyes and take seven, slow deep breaths. Now that you are finished, I have seven affirmations that I would ask that you repeat out loud wherever you are (i.e., at home, on your job, in the car, by yourself, or even with friends/loved ones). You may be asking why I want you to say this out loud.

Well, I am so glad you did!

The truth is that there is power in your words. Proverbs 18:21 (KJV) says, "Death and life are in the power of the tongue: and they that love it shall eat the fruit thereof." This means that the blessings of your life have been waiting on you to speak them into fruition. So let's practice, repeat after me:

Reigning in Royalty

If you're reading this declare this out loud

7 I AM's

I AM a reflection of the beauty of God!

I AM fearfully and wonderfully made!

I AM loved by God!

I AM chosen by God!

I AM an heir of His inheritance!

I AM a carrier of His glory!

I AM destined to win!

Reigning in Royalty

There is nothing more gratifying, than to know that the one true and living God – that created this earth and everything in it – wants to involve you in His plan for humanity.

Too often we see ourselves as a mistake and think that because we messed up, we cannot be used by Him. This has to be the furthest from the truth. When you examine the Bible, you will see that some of the most successful people messed up the most.

Moses was a murderer, David was an adulterer, Solomon was an idolater, and Peter denied our Savior, Jesus Christ. We are not exempt! We have all done things that were not pleasing to God, but glory be to God, that is not who we are. He does not call us contrary to what the Word says we are; when He looks at us, He sees Jesus.

This is why you had to repeat the seven affirmations. There are so many more you could have said, but we have to start somewhere. Speaking of which, here is my story before I said "yes" to God and before He changed my life.n waiting on you to speak them into fruition. So let's practice, repeat after me:

Growing up as a young girl, I was filled with the idea that I would have the "American Dream." The American Dream being I would marry Mr. Right, we would have beautiful kids, and we would live in this gorgeous house that had the white, picket fence.

However, they did not share with me the process it would take to get me to my "happily ever after." This unrealistic notion set me up to be vulnerable as I encountered the situations and temptations of life. In turn, I entertained individuals that did not value themselves, and because they did not value themselves, they did not value me.

I gave of myself and they would use me for whatever they desired to use me for. Once they got out of me what they wanted to get out of me, they would leave me and I would be left alone feeling empty, defeated, and unloved. I would continue searching for love in all of the wrong places and the cycle would continue.

I was not a promiscuous young lady, but as the cards were dealt to me would have it, I found myself face-to-face with the threat of having an incurable disease. How could this happen to me, God? I was not out there! Just the thought of having an incurable disease allowed me to fall subject to the lies that the enemy was pumping in my head.

Reigning in Royalty

He subtly said to me, "You are never going to get married! You are never going to have any children! That dream that you had, it's over and gone!" I allowed Satan's words to rest in my head. He set up camp and had a field day. I believed every single thing that he was saying to me. I slipped into a minor depression.

I did not want to eat, I did not want to go anywhere. I did not even want to perform menial day-to-day tasks. I was having a pity party if you will. BUT GOD!!! One day, the Spirit of the Lord spoke to me.

I heard Him say, "Get up!" It was like He was reading my card. He asked me if I was going to continue to waddle in my pain or if I was going to get up/rise up and walk in His ways. God asked me to do something that day, that I never knew how to do…TRUST Him! Now, I knew who God was because I spent my days in church hearing/learning all about Him, but I did not have a personal relationship with Him.

I did not know Him for myself. I only knew what people told me about Him. It was weird to know that I did not know how to trust God. I grew up in church. I sang all about Him. I served in the church. How could I not trust Him? Little did I know, trusting God is so much more than lip service and just saying, "I trust you, Lord!" In that moment I said, "Yes God! I have no other choice but to trust You."

I was at my wits end and had nothing else to lose. After this encounter, I got up and I learned how to develop my relationship with God. I dove into His Word and He began to share with me that I was the apple of His eye (Psalm 17:8); that He loves me with an everlasting love (Jeremiah 31:3); that I was fearfully and wonderfully made (Psalm 139:14); and that there was nothing that I could do that would separate me from His love (Romans 8:38). These Scriptures changed my life and helped me to realize that God was waiting on me to return back to Him, the lover of my soul.

When one is learning who he/she is, and trying to grasp the totality of his/her identity, there is a time of evaluation and pronouncement. This is the time where you must identify those qualities that make up your character,challenge those things that are not like God, and come to an inner conclusion as to who you really are. Once you are convinced as to who you really are, you make it known by affirming what you choose to answer to.

Throughout this process of identification, there may be times where you will want to convert back to what is most familiar, as getting to know the real you can be daunting task. However, I want to encourage you to not give up until God has completed the work within you (Philippians 1:6).

Reigning in Royalty

Let's take Paul, formerly Saul of Tarsus, for instance. Paul had an encounter with the Lord on his way to Damascus (Acts 9). On his way to Damascus, Paul experienced a light that shined so brightly that it temporarily blinded him. While blind, Paul was led the rest of the way to Damascus, as unbeknownst to him, God had preordained someone to tell him who he was. Simultaneously, Ananias – a servant of the Lord, had a vision. God told him specifically where to go and that he would find Saul there praying.

When Ananias arrived, it was just as God said. God told Ananias that Saul was His chosen vessel and that he would bear His name (identity). When Ananias arrived, he called Saul "Brother." At that very moment, the scales fell from Saul's eyes – his eyes were opened to the things of the Spirit (evaluation), and he arose and was baptized (pronouncement). So, this passage reminds us that it is not what you have done in the past that matters most, but your ability to re-evaluate, repent, and respond to the call of God on your life. You are a child of the Most High God!

After conversion, comes challenge to see if you really meant that which was confessed. Not every day after my conversion has been easy; it certainly has not been a cake walk, nor has it been like laying on a bed of roses. God does not promise it would be so. I have had trial after trial and temptation after temptation; but, every single time God provides a way of escape (1Corinthians 10:13). Our trials serve a purpose. James 1:3-4 (AMP) says, "Be assured, that the testing of your faith [through experience] produces endurance [leading to spiritual maturity, and inner peace]. And let endurance have its perfect result and do a thorough work, so that you may be perfect and completely developed [in your faith], lacking in nothing."

Nevertheless, in the midst of my trials, I am reminded daily of who I am in Christ and to whom I belong to. God reminded me that I am valuable. I may not be valuable to man, but I am priceless to Him. I went from being vulnerable to valuable; from rejected to redeemed; from frightened to full of power; from skeptical to secure; from belittled to beautiful; from condemned to chosen; and from rebellious to royalty.

Now that I believe in my value, people must respect the value that I know I possess. Satan definitely intended for my situation to take me out. On the contrary, I now have a gift and a Godfidence that no one can take away; that gift is my personal relationship with Christ.

I want to encourage you today that regardless of your story, whatever it may be, that God is waiting for you to open up your heart so that He can come into you. He's waiting on you to say "Yes," so He can give you every blessing that He has lined up for you. There is absolutely nothing that you have done that could make Him love you less.

He already knows the very details of your life; he even knows the very numbers of hairs on your head; as a matter of fact, he knows your thoughts before you even think them (Psalm 139). Guess what? He still calls you blessed; he still calls you friend (John 15:15). He longs to show us grace and mercy! All we have to do is repent and rely on His Word. Never forget to show yourself grace, because we all have sinned and fallen short of the glory of God (Romans 3:23).The overall purpose of this chapter is to share the fact that God has predestined you to Reign in Royalty. Reigning (ruling) requires recognition of the levels that you have attained.

Reigning in Royalty

Here are the lessons I have learned about myself. I can confidently say that

I am powerful
I am loved
I am beautiful
I have value
I am chosen
I am royalty.

I have been given the right to declare my destiny.
I am called to help other women identify their worth and beauty. I am also called to boldly minister God's Word to the nations. I am an Administrator – my purpose is to outline plans that are easy to execute, for both individuals and organizations. I am an Exhorter – I have been called to fulfill 1 Thessalonians 5:11,

"Encourage each other while it is yet today." I am a Discerner – I am able to test the spirit of a matter. I am a Giver – I understand that I have been blessed to be a blessing.

Reigning in Royalty

Finally, I am a Leader – I am called to lead and influence the people of God's kingdom.

I now understand how God sees me. Therefore, I understand that my sole purpose is to magnify who He is in the presence of others. As I focus completely on Him, He will also make my name known in the market place. He is opening doors and speaking engagements for me. I will mentor His people face-to-face, and I will minister at venues that only He can open for me. I commit to keeping my scheduled time with God and remaining a student of His Word.

I will continue seeking to participate in seminars and classes that will continue to push me in my next dimension. I have inspected my grid. These are the people that are assigned to my life: my corner, my circle, and my cloud. God has connected me with a God-fearing husband that keeps me accountable; He has blessed me with a group sisters who have proven that their intention is to push me to do what God has called me to do; He has also blessed me with a wonderful mentor, Pastor Khalilah Olokunola.

I will continue to surround myself with people who are walking in the same direction that I am walking. If they don't want to grow, they must go! I will intentionally stay away from those that serve as distractions and lead me away from the path that God has destined for me.

Reigning in Royalty

After this, I am confident in who I am. I will no longer be a captive or a slave to fear. I cannot keep my mouth closed, for He has made me to be His mouthpiece.

My identity is connected to His will for my life, and I give Him all of the glory for being able to even participate in a project that will change lives and advance the kingdom of God.

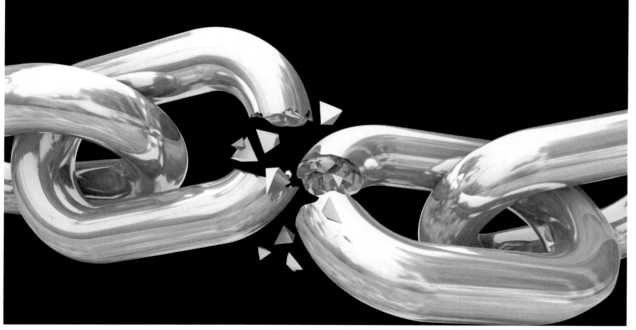

Reigning in Royalty

In closing, I would like to thank you so very much for your support of this ministry. Without you, our gifts would be null and void. It has truly been a glorious time and I pray that you have received a blessing – just as I have – from the testimony that was shared. You may be broken, but you are not beyond repair. Readjust your Crown, Realign your Focus, and then Reign in Royalty because that's what you have been called to do!

 I am going to end with a quick prayer and the chorus of a song by Dante Bowe that is truly fitting:Father thank you for this time of impartation. I pray that it has blessed the hearts of your people.May every word point your people back to you; may it accomplish that which you've set out to accomplish. May it not return to you void. Father, I've tried so hard to see why You'd choose someone like me to carry Your victory. Perfection could never earn it; You've given what we don't deserve.

You take the broken things and raise them to glory. You are my champion! Giants fall when you stand undefeated; every battle You've won. I am who You say I am! You crown me with confidence. I am seated, in the heavenly place, undefeated, with the One who has conquered it all. Amen!May the Lord make His face shine upon you, and be gracious to you (Numbers 6:24)

Reigning in Royalty

Chapter 4

Bright Women

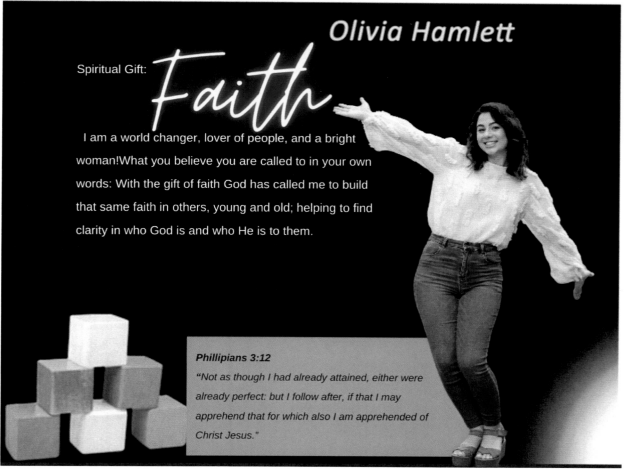

Olivia Hamlett

Spiritual Gift: *Faith*

I am a world changer, lover of people, and a bright woman!What you believe you are called to in your own words: With the gift of faith God has called me to build that same faith in others, young and old; helping to find clarity in who God is and who He is to them.

Phillipians 3:12
"Not as though I had already attained, either were already perfect: but I follow after, if that I may apprehend that for which also I am apprehended of Christ Jesus."

God loves you!

It does not matter what you have done or are doing, what you may think about yourself, or what others may say about you. You are so loved by God! There are gifts inside of you; someone is waiting on your voice, your books, your prayers, your testimony. In the world we live in it can be so easy to allow everything around you distract you from everything in you. The way we perceive the world can sometimes alter the way we perceive ourselves. It may seem like negativity speaks louder than all the positive aspects around you and in you. Don't let the enemy take your mind! You have to combat condemning thoughts with who God says you are. You are loved, you are powerful, you are a child of God! When you feel and believe that you are less than any of those things, it is hard to stand up and speak against them. But, you have to, you have to get up. You have to push through the pain to learn the purpose. You can do it, you are so much stronger than you think.

Bright Women

If you're reading this declare this out loud

7 I AM's

I am loved

I am powerful

I am bold

I am courageous

I am called

I am bright

I am a child of God!

Bright Women

My name is Olivia Hamlett and here is my story. I do not remember much from my childhood. The things I do remember don't always put a smile on my face. I remember living a life filled with anger around me and in me. My parents struggled with getting along creating a lot of disorder in our home; constant fighting, screaming, hatred, disrespect, and loneliness. They eventually got divorced when I was around the age of 9, then things really took a turn. Too many court dates later, my mom lived in a different state and the judge ruled for me and my two siblings to live with my dad. This was a very big transition for my sister, my brother, and I. I was hurt, I felt abandoned, I was scared, I was lonely, and I was angry. Those feelings only grew as I got older, eventually creating a numbness within my heart. Shortly after my parents got divorced my siblings, my dad, and me moved into my grandparents house. From there a routine was developed; I lived with my dad for most of the year and I visited my mom during the summer, spring break, and every other Christmas. Year after year went by and numbness. continued to fill me.

Nothing ever seemed to satisfy the people around me, especially my family. Titles such as psycho, and whore were sometimes given to me from people I would least expect it from. All I wanted was someone to make me feel like I was doing a good job. Instead, I walked around trying to fill a hole with quick sand; no matter what I did I always managed to still sink. Never being good enough allowed self condemnation to rule my life. I was constantly evaluating myself, wondering if I was kind enough, or said the right thing, or made the right decision. Always wondering if I pleased the other person. Most of the time I failed myself, which pushed me into a dark tunnel of self hate. This led to me placing myself into toxic situations in the hope of feeling loved in some kind of way.

Bright Women

The last five years is where most of my pain and condemnation weighed on me the most. I grew up knowing of a God but having a relationship with God was foreign. About two years ago is when I really started chasing after Him. God enabled me to truly say that all my pain, anger, and fear had a purpose. God showed me so much grace and love and began to change my heart's desires. I will never be the same and I am so grateful to God.continued to fill me.

Bright Women

From Pain to Purpose

I went from:

Dark to Determined

Lonely to Lively

Bonded to Brave

Low to Loved

Hurt to Hopeful

Broken to Bright

Condemned to Confident.

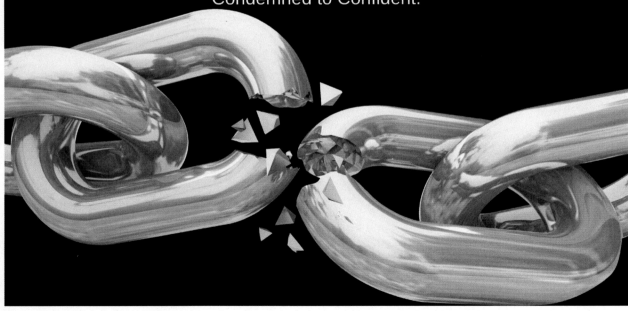

Bright Women

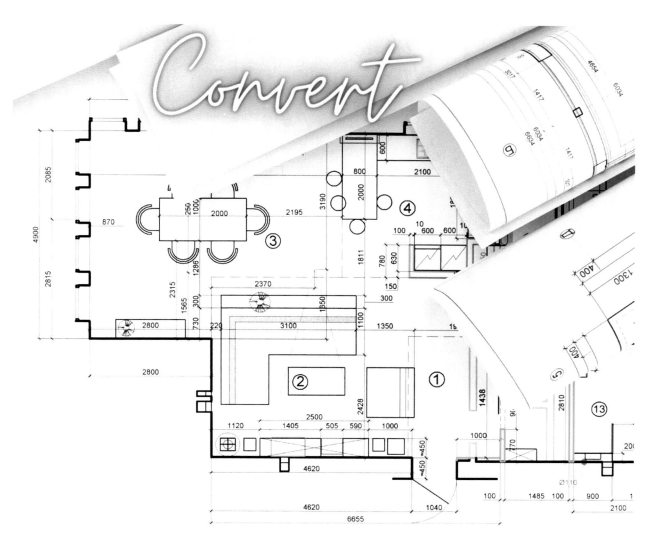

Through it all God has given me a new perspective. God has shown me what real love is, He has filled that hole of emptiness I had inside of me. I can now truly and whole heartily tell you that I am a Bright Woman! I am loved, I am called, I am valiant, I am daring, I am powerful, I am worthy, I am light, I am a child of God!

1　　　　　　2　　　　　　　　　　　　3　　　　4

There is absolutely nothing that can separate you from God's love. It says it in Romans 8:39 "Nothing can separate me from God's love." Nothing really means nothing! Be bold in believing this, speak it until you feel it. Stand courageously as the strong being you are and let nothing get in the way of you and God. I dare you to pray this prayer; Dear God, I thank you for your never ending love, your grace, and your mercy.

I surrender my life to you completely and ask that you help me see me the way you see me. I need you God and I am ready to walk into who you say I am. I thank you God for all the ways that you will help me. All the glory goes to you.

In Jesus' name I pray, amen

Bright Women

Chapter 5

I am a child of the most high God

Christie Washington

Spiritual Gift: *Service*

Child of God , Sister , Friend ,
Overcomer, Encourager

Philippians 4:13

says I can do all things through Christ
who strengthens me. not only do I
believe that but I stand on it

I am a Child of God

Connect

The gift of serving is the divine strength or ability to do small or great tasks in working for the overall good of the body of Christ.I believe I am called to encourage, minister to and help those less fortunate. Those going through the ups and downs in life while giving them hope that there's light at the end of the tunnel. Assuring them that if God did it for me then He will do it for them.

I want to encourage somebody today who can not see the light at the end of the tunnel. No matter how dark it may seem you just have to keep pushing towards the light. It's been plenty of times when I just wanted to throw in the towel but this God that I heard of but didn't really know had a plan for my life and I was running from it trying to do everything Christie's way. Now looking back from then to now I know that this God that I didn't know kept and covered me all of these years before I ever knew who he was.

I am a Child of God

If you're reading this declare this out loud

7 I AM's

I AM A CHILD OF GOD

I AM MARKED BY THE MAJESTY

I AM FEARFULLY AND WONDERFULLY MADE IN

HIS IMAGE

I AM AN OVERCOMER

I AM A CONQUEROR

I AM BRAVE

I AM ENOUGH

I am a Child of God

My name is Christie Washington and here is my story - Growing up I was a wild child running wild. Living wreck less and getting into any and everything imaginable. Nobody could tell me anything because I had all the answers. I started working at a young age so I was able to pretty much get whatever I wanted whenever I wanted. I was self-centered, hard headed and broken. Carrying around images in my head of my childhood and how rough it was growing up in a single-family home that ended in divorce when I was 5 years old. Fast forward to my teen years , life got real. I started getting into all types of trouble, running with the wrong crowd, and ended up behind bars on numerous occasions. Being put on probation, being violated and getting a gun charge. Yet and still I had all the answers. Later in my twenty's things started to slow down a bit.

I was able to attend college, land a good job and things was on the up and up. But little did I know my life was about to change forever. I was diagnosed with a nerve condition and spinal condition that permanently put me out of work. Now the Christie that was so independent and had it all figured out needed somebody. The tables turned that quick. I had all of the material things anybody could ever want and lost them. There we're times when I couldn't even walk at all I had to crawl. Injection after injection. Procedure after procedure.

My sibling was really the only person I could rely on because everybody else turned their back on me because I wasn't in a position to do anything for them. I've lived in a hotel room for 30 plus days or more because the ones that claimed they loved me turned their back on me.

I am a Child of God

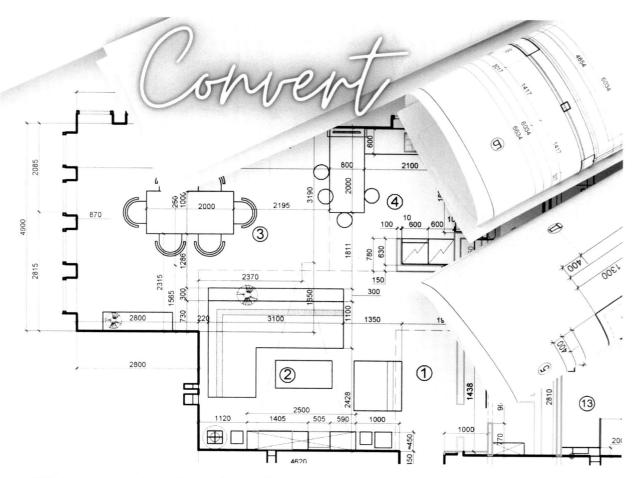

Convert

At that very moment in my darkest time I said yes. I no longer had the strength to fight anymore. I asked God to help me because I couldn't help myself. I was all out of tears, hope and fight. My life took a turn in a whole new direction. I gave my life to Christ. My battle wasn't over though because I still had to fight another 9 years for what was rightfully mine. Now that all the smoke has cleared, I know for a fact that without God reaching down and pulling me up out of that dark place when I cried out, I probably wouldn't be writing this today. God has a funny way of humbling those that know it all. Looking back, I know that God had to crush me to build me. Eliminate people, places and things, and show me that he is the source. And without him I am nothing and never will be. If God can rebuild me and restore me from all of my mess, he can do it for you too.

1   2   3   4

From Pain to Purpose

I went from overwhelmed to overcomer

I went from victim to victor

I went from opposition to opportunity

I went from attacks to elevation

I went from error to order

I went from bitter to better

I went from pain to purpose

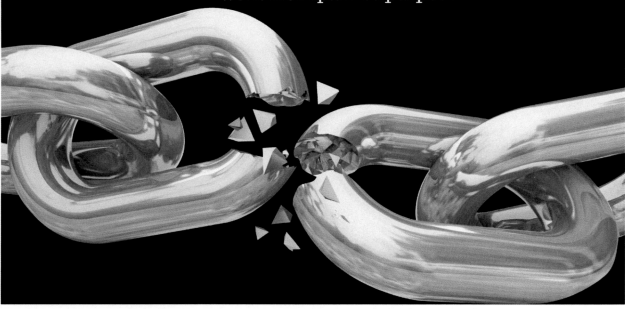

I am a Child of God

Today I am restored and redesigned

Father God I ask that you bless every person reading this prayer. I ask that you change their hearts as well as their mind.

I ask that you instill in them that all things are possible through you God and only you.

I pray that you meet every physical need, emotional need, relational need, financial need and most importantly every spiritual need.

In Jesus Name I Pray Amen.

I am a Child of God

Chapter 6

Terms of Service

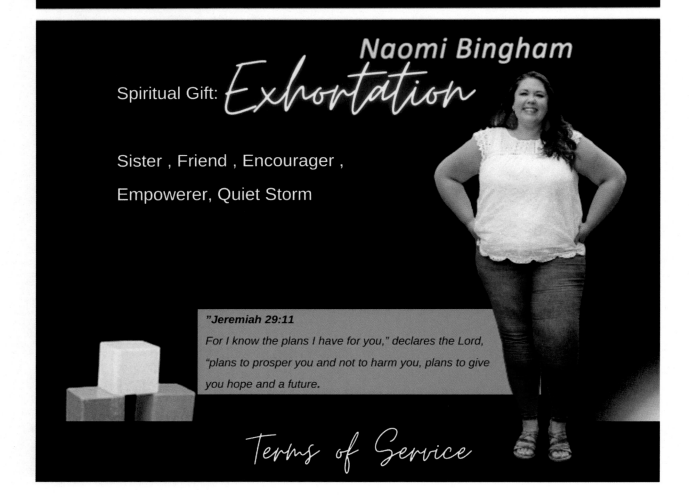

Naomi Bingham

Spiritual Gift: Exhortation

Sister , Friend , Encourager ,
Empowerer, Quiet Storm

"Jeremiah 29:11
For I know the plans I have for you," declares the Lord,
"plans to prosper you and not to harm you, plans to give
you hope and a future.

Terms of Service

I grew up in a very tiny town in central North Carolina but I didn't have the typical small town experience. Most people who grow up in small towns are only exposed to people who look like them, talk like them, act like them, believe like them. I was blessed with a different experience. I lived in the same town and went to the same church from the time I was born until I was in my late 20s. I also attended a private, Christian school until the 9th grade. Hearing those things about me, you may think that there is no way I saw diversity during my formative years, but you would be wrong. Before I was 18 years old, I had encountered, grown up beside, and made friends with people from all walks of life.

From the trailer parks to the ritzy neighborhoods. Individuals with varying physical and mental needs. People of all skin tones. Families from different religious backgrounds.

Young men and women who sold drugs. Students who were failing and those who were soaring scholars. Young women with eating disorders. And even a precious young woman who was forced to have an abortion in order to not be kicked out of her own home.

But never one time did I see myself as better than anyone or think that any of those people were less than me because, as I learned from the time I was young, "Red and yellow, black and white, we are precious in His sight, Jesus loves the little children of the world." I not only heard those words, but saw those actions in the people around me and specifically in my household.

That's why, when I entered a public city high school in 9th grade, I literally had friends in every circle you can think of: the band members, the athletes, the chorus students, the mechanics, the math geniuses, the skater rats, the hacky sack players, the R&B crew, the poets, the introverts, the extroverts, all of them. I struggled with the requirement to belong exclusively to one particular clique or group. I believe we have all been created equally in the presence of God and we bring different gifts, talents, and perspectives to the table.

I would miss out on so many amazing experiences if I believed my way was the only right way to see and do things. What you believe you are called to in your own words.

I believe I am called to empower people to reach their true potential in Him. I am called to help people see who God has created them to be and to be brave enough to step out and be that person. I believe He has also empowered me to reach people of all ages, far and wide; to encourage them; to help them see they are "enough"; to know that there is a reason we are who we are and to see how that translates into who God created us to be and His purpose for our lives.

Terms of Service

Connect

I'm sharing my story with you because I 'm hoping you see that God works in the lives of everyone. I grew up in the church and was given all the tools for success, yet still I didn't KNOW God. It took getting to the place of being alone and "on my own" to really see God for who He is. I hope there are people reading this who, like me, have grown up in the church and have a wealth of knowledge of who He is, but haven't yet had an experience with Him. Have you found that God never turns his back on you? I have.

I knew so much about the Bible but I got to the point where I thought He wouldn't love me anymore because I had done too much wrong. But never one time in the scriptures does it say that we can go too far or do too much wrong that God won't love us. Be encouraged; God hears you. He sees you where you are and knows your heart. You have not gone too far.

You have not drifted away from His grasp. You have not done anything so bad that your heavenly father won't welcome you back into his arms the moment you call upon his name. He loves you. He sees you as his perfect child. He created you to be "stubborn", He calls it "unshakable". He created you to be "unique", He calls it "perfect in His sight". He created you to be "loud", He calls it "bold".

He created you to "not be swayed by others opinions", He calls it "walking in dignity". So don't you ever doubt God's purpose for your life. All those things that others have questioned or degraded you for are the exact things that God will use to raise you up. I have learned that while others took advantage of my caring heart and kindness, God is showing me how to use that kindness to love those who may think they are unlovable.

When others told me to sit down and be quiet because I was just trying to "get attention", God showed me that he gave me the tenacity and gift of exhortation to lift others up.

He has taught me I need to open my mouth more and speak to the broken-hearted to show His love to the world.

Terms of Service

If you're reading this declare this out loud

7 I AM's

I am bold

I am fearless and full of faith

I am tenacious

I am being filled with joy and laughter

I am a bearer of peacel am wanted

I am chosen

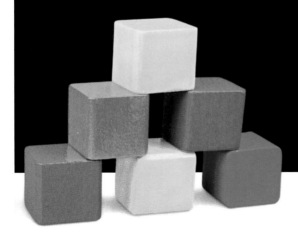

Terms of Service

Confess

My name is Naomi and here is my story. Growing up in the church, I was blessed to have a knowledge of Christ and the Scriptures as a child. I had a firm foundation of scriptural truths and accepted Jesus into my heart at a young age. I even remember having very specific encounters with God as a child. But as I grew older, there were a lot of things I did and didn't do, not based on my love for God but rather my fear of not being a perfect Christian. While I could accept everyone else exactly as they were, I couldn't accept myself as being anything less than perfect. My relationship with Christ went from being heart focused, to being head focused.

I was so caught up in what a "perfect Christian" should and should not do that I lost sight of having an actual relationship with God. That led to a lot of guilt when I made wrong choices and a feeling of condemnation regardless of what I did. I was always second guessing my actions, even when I could tell the Spirit was leading me to do something, like encourage someone or pray for someone. I stopped using my talents and gifts because I constantly felt that I was less than perfect and in my mind someone who's not perfect should not be doing spiritual things.

During this time of questioning my gifts and not walking in my purpose, my world fell apart. The pastor whom I had known since birth, retired and moved away. The church I attended since birth, dissolved

The marriage I was in hit rock bottom and ended. And my mother and brother moved away. So here I was in a world I had never known. Alone, betrayed, rejected, and no idea how to move forward. That's where I really met God. It was in this place that He started showing me who He really is. I was living on my own for the very first time in my life.

I was scared, overwhelmed, and had no idea what I was doing. But it was in those moments of not knowing, God came in and showed me His plan. There were times I had no food in the house and didn't know how I would pay my bills, every single time God showed up and made a way. I was evicted from my apartment and didn't know where I would sleep. Twice in my life, I shared a room with the child of a friend until I could get back on my feet. It was all very humbling, really. I like to think that I can handle everything by myself, yet I found over and over again that I not only needed God but I needed people too..

There were times where the pain was too much to bear and I would cry out to Him in the night. He met me there every single time. I can't tell you the number of nights I cried myself to sleep but would wake with such a sweet peace. This is where my relationship with Him started growing. This is where I learned that my relationship with God wasn't just Him telling me what to do and not to do. But it was also me sharing my heart with Him. During this season, I found that He needed to hear my cries, and needed me to speak out loud what I needed from him.

Terms of Service

If you had asked me if I was a Christian before all this, I would have said without a doubt, "yes I am". But looking back I realize that although I was a "Christian" I didn't have a full relationship with God. I would listen to some feel good songs, I would get convicted from time to time and change my ways; many times only for a moment then I would revert back to my old habits.

I would hear a good word and try to be a better person. For some reason though, I never accepted that a relationship with God was a 2 way street. I learned that I had to be vulnerable with God. I started telling him how I felt, about everything. I started talking to him like he was my best friend, sitting in the room beside me. There were nights I yelled at God; asked him "why?"; told Him I was done with life; begged Him to take me out of this world because I just couldn't take it anymore. I told Him all the good things too. I would thank Him for the wonderful things He had done for me. I learned that a two way street still doesn't require me to be perfect, just honest.

This is where He started showing me that in order to fulfill my purpose, there were some things I would have to accept. He started issuing my terms of service and the promises He would stand on when those terms were fulfilled. "

Terms of service" is an agreement between a service provider and a person who wants to use that service . The person must agree to abide by the terms of service in order to use the offered service. His promises are found in the Word and the authenticity cannot be denied. I have to accept that things won't always be perfect.

I have to accept that some days, it will get messy. He said there would be bad days, and we know that there would be good days too; but when I trust in Him and lean not on my own understanding; when I acknowledge Him in all things, He WILL make straight my paths. (Prov. 3:5-6)

I have to accept that I am fearfully and wonderfully made and I have been created for a purpose. I must accept that those things I see about myself that cause me to cringe, make God smile.I think I'm loud and talk too much yet He created me to exhort others; to bring healing with my words. While yet in my mother's womb, He was carving out His plans for me. Those plans include pain and persecution; nights of darkness and joy that is found in the morning. His plan for me is not to frolic in the meadows oblivious to the struggles that plague my brothers and sisters in this world; but for me to live my life with my eyes wide open so that I am not blind to the battle that is raging around me.

I must also accept that I do not always know what is best for me. Jeremiah 29:11 says it best, "For I (GOD) know the plans I have for you; plans to prosper you and not to harm you; plans to give you hope and a future." When I lean not on my own understanding and I surrender my plans to Him, the result will always be a hope and a future.

Terms of Service

From Pain to Purpose

I went from FearFULL to FaithFULL

I was once REJECTED but now I am RECEIVED

I went from BROKEN to BEAUTIFUL

I was CONFINED but now I am COMPELLED

I felt UNWORTHY, yet He UNVEILED His plans for me.

I felt ABANDONED, but He said I am ADOPTED

I once was full of BLEMISHES and now I am full of BLESSINGS

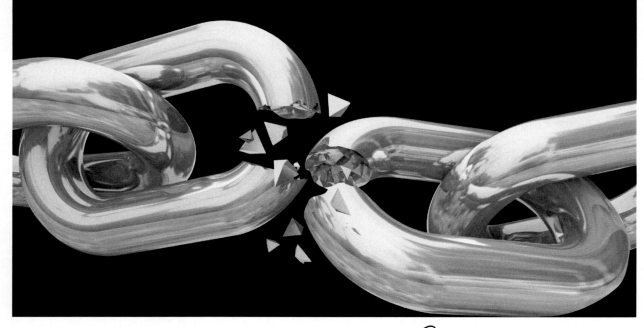

Terms of Service

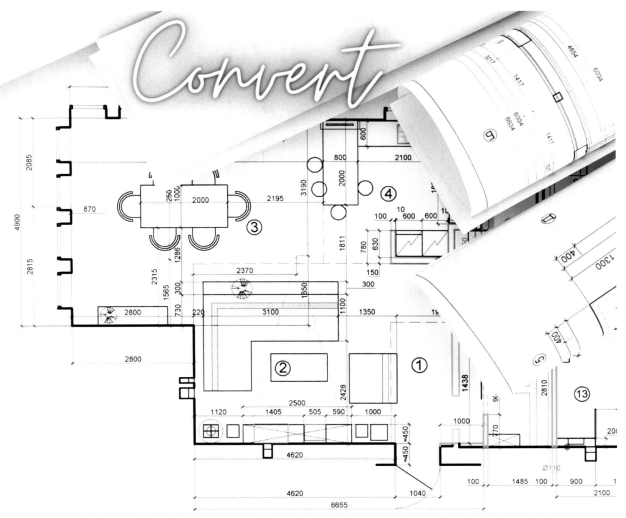

Today I am walking in His grace and I know that He has a plan for my life. Every single trial and tribulation that I have endured is for a purpose. It is so I can understand where others are coming from and encourage them that all is not lost. I am still not perfect by man's standards but I know that I am perfect in the eyes of my Father. He is still working on me and that gives me hope!

1   2   3   4

This could be your story as well. God has a definite purpose for your life. He designed you with an actual plan in mind. You are no accident. Your journey is not a mistake. Yes, you have endured pain and heartache. Sure, you have made decisions that you knew you shouldn't have made. And there have been times you turned away from God because you knew you would disappoint him with your choices. But guess what? He has never turned his back on you. In 2 Peter 3:9 it says "The Lord is not slow to fulfill his promise as some count slowness, but is patient toward you, not wishing that any should perish, but that all should reach repentance." Our father wants us to walk in our purpose. He has no desire to leave us hanging and out in the world on our own with no direction on how to turn.

He has chosen you to tell your story so that someone else may see his mighty works and be led to Him as well. Are you ready to share your story? Are you ready to help someone else see the "Christ in you, the hope of glory"? Col. 1:27 Because what really matters is not WHAT is in us but rather WHO is in us. What do you want others to see when they look at you? I know what we see when we look in the mirror. A bundle of bad choices, a myriad of mistakes, a heap of hurt and it goes on and on. But what if, for one moment, we could see what we look like when others see us through the hope of glory? When glory is present, now others can see what God brought you through, they can see his redemption and salvation in your life. Others can now see that God has taken you from mistakes to a mansion. Glory to God!

So let's start looking in this mirror of our life and state the things that are true.·

"God loves me" Psalm 36:7 "How precious is your steadfast love, O God! The children of mankind take refuge in the shadow of your wings."·

"I belong to God" 1 John 4:4 4 You, dear children, are from God and have overcome them, because the one who is in you is greater than the one who is in the world."·

God is my protector" Romans 8:31–32 "What then shall we say to these things? If God is for us, who can be against us? He who did not spare his own son but gave him up for us all, how will he not also graciously give us all things?"·

"God does not stay angry with me." Micah 7:18-20 (The Message) Where is the god who can compare with you—wiping the slate clean of guilt, Turning a blind eye, a deaf ear, to the past sins of your purged and precious people? You don't nurse your anger and don't stay angry long, for mercy is your specialty. That's what you love most. And compassion is on its way to us. You'll stamp out our wrongdoing. You'll sink our sins to the bottom of the ocean. You'll stay true to your word to Father Jacob and continue the compassion you showed Grandfather Abraham—Everything you promised our ancestors   from a long time ago.·   "

Terms of Service

There is a plan for my life– Psalm 37:23-24 "The steps of a man are established by the Lord, when he delights in his way; though he falls, he shall not be cast headlong, for the Lord upholds his hand."·

"I will trust him with each step I take" Proverbs 3:5-6 "Trust in the LORD with all your heart, and do not lean on your own understanding. In all your ways acknowledge him, and he will make straight your paths

Dear heavenly Father,

I come to you now on behalf of the person reading this right now. I ask you to surround them with your presence and let this heart know that you are near. Jesus, we thank you for the amazing things you have done in our lives; how you got us to this point. There is never an accident when it comes to your timing so we know that this moment is ordained by you. We acknowledge that every situation and circumstance has led us to this specific moment in time and we thank you for it. God I lift my sisters and brothers to you in prayer and ask that you would speak to this heart right now. That where there is loneliness, you will bring comfort. Where there is confusion, you will bring peace. I ask right now that where there is hurt and agony and suffering, that you will bring your healing balm of Gilead and pour it on this spirit.

God, we believe that this person has a purpose. We know that you have ordained them for greatness. We are convinced that you have a plan and have ordered their steps while they were yet in the womb. Sometimes in life we take detours and hit roadblocks, yet the moment we turn our eyes to you, you will always make the way plain to us and lead us to our destination. Father we thank you for your mercy and grace. We thank you for the wonders of your majesty. Jesus we thank you that all we must do is ask, and you will show us the way. Lord we lift each and every soul that is reading this and lay them at your feet. We ask that you will open their eyes to the truth that is you and that you will reveal your purpose to their spirit. Jesus we thank you that "there is none like you.

No one else can touch our hearts like you do. We could search for all eternity and find there is none like you" (Songwriters: Lenny Leblanc). We are thankful for the words of Philippians 4 which states "Do not be anxious about anything, but in everything by prayer and supplication with thanksgiving let your requests be made known to God.

And the peace of God, which surpasses all understanding, will guard your hearts and your minds in Christ Jesus." We have no reason to be anxious, we are not called to worry. We are designed with a purpose and all we must do is ask. Thank you Lord for what you are revealing to this heart right now. Glory to your name for the work you are doing in this life. We praise you and bless you. In Jesus' name. Amen.

Terms of Service

Chapter 7

Pressing forward with Grace!

Spiritual Gift: *Helps*

Carlette Grissett

Essential Worker , Woman of God ,

Forerunner

Proverbs 31:8-9

Speak up for those who cannot speak for themselves, for the rights of all who are destitute. Speak up and judge fairly; defend the rights of the poor and needy.

Moving Forward with Grace

In this season, I'm doing things that I never could have imagined me doing. I've prayed for a change, a new journey, a new walk with God! When I saw Pastor KO's post about The Breakthrough Blueprint Master Class, this was it! I needed something, I needed to connect and learn from my sisters in Christ. Even Though I didn't have the money like that, I signed up anyway, and paid it, and here I am...BLESSED !

I walked out on faith, I wanted to get something out of the class, but what got, I could have never imagined! So yes, I'm Moving Forward with Grace! Last month the ladies and I took a spiritual gift test. I found out my five top Spiritual gifts. I was very shocked at a few, but there was one gift that I knew I always had, this was the gift of Helps.

This gift, the gift of Helps, is the divine strength or ability to work in a supportive role for the accomplishment of a task in Christan Ministry, with the ability to often see the need before others do. All Christians are called to help others in need, yet some are clearly more gifted in this role than others. Looking back over my life, I can truly say that I'm more gifted than others. Working in the healthcare field for 20 plus years, I' ve seen a lot. It has taught me how precious life is. So as I grow in my Christian walk, I'm going to expand in this spiritual gift of Helps, because it is who I am, It is what I've been called to do

I'm sharing my store in hope that it can help someone. There were times when I wanted to quit, because yes life was hard. I use to question God, why me? Why is it easy for other people and I have to work harder and struggle at it (life). I'm not going to lie, I was mad! I've always been a shy person, I've always tried to do right by people, but in return, they didn't do right by me.

Sitting here looking back over my life, it has made me who I am! I'm here to encourage you, don't give up! I gave my life to God, Easter Sunday 2002, baptized May 28, 2006.

It was the best decision I could have made. I still struggled though, but God was there to pick me up, and he has made ways, out of no way! Brings tears to my eyes thinking about the goodness of God! God alone has made me who I am!

Moving Forward with Grace

If you're reading this declare this out loud

7 I AM's

I am strong

I am worthy

I am beautiful

I am smart

I am helps

I am wonderfully made

I am what God says I am

Pressing forward in Grace

Confess

My name is Carlette, and this is my story. I was raised on the Northside of Wilmington, NC, in the Rankin Terrance Projects. The only girl, middle child, in a single parent (mother) household. I struggled a lot, I was a very shy kid growing up, this played a role in school. I hated school! I just couldn't keep up, this led me to repeat the 1st grade. My mom said I wasn't ready for the 2nd grade.

This was very heart breaking for a child to hear, I couldn't go on to another grade with my classmates...I felt dumb! Throughout my elementary years, I was in all kinds of labs, these were placed in the schools, to help you in your class. With the help of these labs, I managed to get out of elementary school. Then there was Junior High (showing my age), same struggles, but this is where I was labeled! Basic Math, Basic English, and so on. The fact that I was in these classes and still failing. I attended summer school twice in those three years.

I couldn't comprehend the school work. By the Grace of God I managed to get to High School, a new school, but still basic! Let me go back for a moment and tell you about my maternal grandmother, Parry Corbett- Canty, and the reason I never gave up.

My grandmother dropped out of school in the 3rd grade, and all ways would say, how she wished she could go back to school. When she died I made it my mission to finish for her! Growing up there really wasn't any talk of going to college,

Moving Forward with Grace

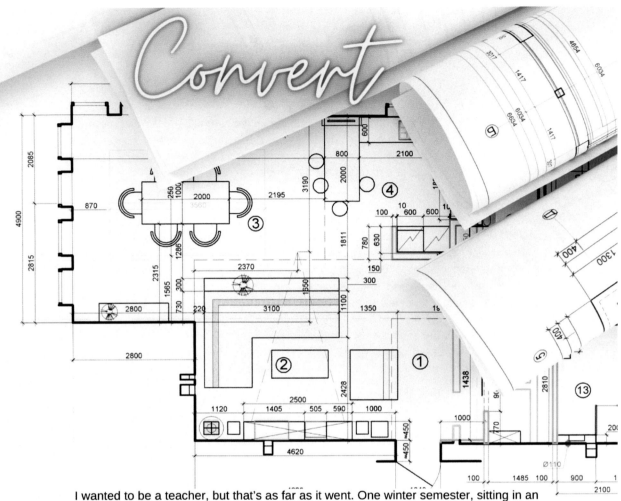

Convert

I wanted to be a teacher, but that's as far as it went. One winter semester, sitting in an elective class with all seniors, they were talking about college, I want to go to college! I felt it was too late, I never took any college ready classes, nor the SAT, ACT. I managed to graduate, by the grace of God. I signed up to attend the community college, I was proud of myself, I passed the classes I was taking. I applied to Morris College, two years there, was doing well. I had to study more, but passed my classes there too! Then life happened, dropped out. Didn't go back until 13 years later, I received my degree as an Associate of Applied Science Degree in Medical Assisting, at Miller- Motte College. ! Ten years from that,

I am now a Junior at Fayetteville State University, and will be graduating in December 2021, with a degree in Sociology! So I can't give up, just look where God has taken me from! God's Grace! God made me more than basic, that's why I'm Moving Forward with Grace!

From Pain to Purpose

I went from shy to confidence

I went from timid to bold.

I went from failure to success.

I went from basic classes to college courses.

I went from hating school to loving school.

I went from hating myself to loving myself.

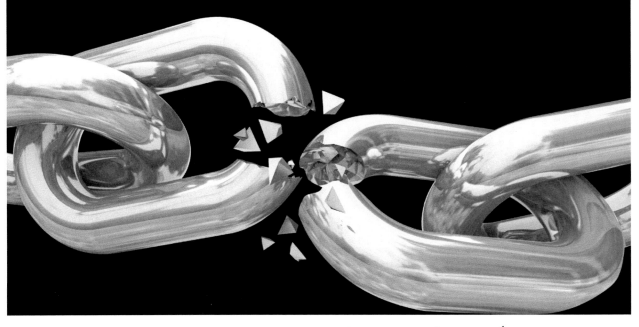

Moving Forward with Grace

Today

 I Am Strong

I Am Beautiful

 I Am Awesome

I Am Wonderfully Made

 I Am Smart

 I Am What God Says I Am

You can be too….

 Never give up, God has a plan for you, even when you can't see it yourself! Yet what we suffer now, is nothing compared to the glory he will reveal to use later. Romans 8:18   I hope this has blessed you in some way, and I pray you put God first in all you do

Dear Lord;

May your light illuminate my life, and your guidance bring direction. Lord you are our hiding place in the time of distress. We turn to you now, seeking comfort from the world, be present in our struggles. Never let us part from you. Amen

Moving Forward with Grace

Chapter 8

"Empowered through Pain"

Kayleigh Keithline

Spiritual Gift: *Exhortation*

Encourager , Counselor

2nd Timothy 1:7

For God has not given us a spirit of fear but of power love and a sound mind". I love the scripture because I can wake up in the morning and declare it over my life daily. This scripture helps me to ground myself and remind me that fear has no hold over my life. Depression, anxiety and negative thoughts are not of God.

Empowered through Pain

I believe God has called me to empower other women through their pain. He is calling me to show other women that they can use their pain as fuel to reach their full potential. Your pain has purpose. You choose your direction. Life is all about the choices you make. You can allow your pain to defeat and define you or you can allow it to empower and encourage you. Its hard! Trust me I know. No one said the process would be easy. It can be at times full blown war, but God has created you to be a solider. You also have a mighty army behind you. You must prepare yourself to step on the battlefield daily. Speak the word over yourself. Create a circle of people who empower you and share some of your goals (we'll talk more later about how important your circle is.

In September of 2018 hurricane Florence hit and we lost everything yet again. Our house was under 3 feet of water. We lost clothes, cars, pictures…everything. Again I tell you But God! He sustained us. We went to the hurricane shelter and strangers love started pouring in. It wasn't people I knew(however some definitely helped!) it was the community. Toys, clothes and food was important in those first couple of weeks. Fast forward the story- by the end of October we were in a new home. While in the shelter I struggled with thoughts daily with "God how are you going to fix this?" I just got my kids back and now I lose my house again? There's all this damage in our city, so many people have lost their homes God how will you find us a new one? He delivered. We moved in with nothing. We slept in the floor with the blankets we had. The new question was God I've worked so hard for everything I had how in the world will you replace it? We have nothing. No beds, couches, TVs, nothing. I even thought this right here is to big for God. We might get a dish or two but we most certainly wont get a house full of furniture right? Oh what a awesome God he is! See when we were in the shelter I happened to share my story with one of the workers that came in to help.

There were hundreds of people in that shelter. Tons of families. She called me within a week of moving into our home. She said hey girl have yall gotten any donations for your house yet? I said no maam. Ok will you be home tomorrow? Yes. Ok well I'm having something delivered to you I just need you to sign for it. Ok no problem. Boy was I not ready for God to blow my mind. When God says he will give exceedingly and abundantly he does just that. I honestly expected a donated couch. Well it was more than just a donated couch. Her brother wanted to bless someone after the hurricanes devastation and was looking for a way to give back. The truck showed up and I signed for it. When they opened the truck I dropped to my knees. It was a whole house full of furniture. I mean every room. Bunk beds for the children, a toddler bed, a full bedroom set for me etc..

I couldn't believe it! The story doesn't end there. This woman showed up the next day with tvs, a game system, gift cards, blankets for the kids and the list goes on. God has truly sustained me. Its so hard to see Gods hand when your in the middle of the storm. When you can't see him and you can't hear him how in the world can you trust him? God why in the world do these battles keep coming? Make it stop! At times it feels that you can barely keep your head above water. If I'm your child and you love me why am I experiencing so much pain? Because my child if I don't plant you how will you grow? See I had to be deeply planted, fertilized and watered before I could begin to grow. I am a very stubborn plant.

Empowered through Pain

Fear, abandonment, rejection, self-esteem issues, depression, overeating to ease the pain, anxiety, teen pregnancy, 3 "baby daddies" (two of which were drug dealers), homelessness times 3, abuse, neglect, sexual assault, promiscuity, domestic violence, 3 children with "high needs", losing custody of my children to DSS. The list goes on. But God! He has sustained me through each and every difficult situation. There are times when I look back and can't help but shout. Its nothing but his grace and mercy that has sustained me. There was a time when I became so overwhelmed I allowed my fear to overpower me. I wasn't focused on God and I certainly wasn't trusting him to help.

I believed, I prayed, I most definitely knew he was there but I wasn't seeking him. I allowed DSS to convince me to voluntarily place both of my boys in therapeutic foster care due to severe behavioral concerns. One thing led to another and within 6 months they forcefully took custody.

I was defeated. Embarrassed, ashamed. Every thing I fought against was now becoming me. I remember the pain being so difficult that I would lay in the floor with my daughters blanket and cry myself to sleep. See this was a pain unlike anything I had ever felt before. I had to grieve the loss of my children but they weren't really gone. I had to listen to the judgement of others around me. In that moment though I had a choice. I could a- throw in the towel and give up or B fight like hell. No one explains to you the process of loosing your children and how to get them back.

No one walks you through the details. It was the hardest battle I've ever fought in my life. The process takes forever. Looking back I can see Gods hand in all of the situation. I was broken for sure but it was graceful. His favor was all over me. It usually takes months before you can begin unsupervised visitations with your kids. I lost custody December 1, 2017. By the end of January I was in the beginning stages of unsupervised visitations. By March the children were spending the weekend. By April they were able to spend a majority of their week with me and in May they were officially home. Before they were removed we were staying in a homeless shelter due to a water main break at our previous residence. God provided a new home for us in December(the day after I lost custody!)

Empowered through Pain

In September of 2018 hurricane Florence hit and we lost everything yet again. Our house was under 3 feet of water. We lost clothes, cars, pictures…everything. Again I tell you But God! He sustained us. We went to the hurricane shelter and strangers love started pouring in. It wasn't people I knew(however some definitely helped!) it was the community. Toys, clothes and food was important in those first couple of weeks. Fast forward the story- by the end of October we were in a new home. While in the shelter I struggled with thoughts daily with "God how are you going to fix this?"

I just got my kids back and now I lose my house again? There's all this damage in our city, so many people have lost their homes God how will you find us a new one? He delivered. We moved in with nothing. We slept in the floor with the blankets we had. The new question was God I've worked so hard for everything I had how in the world will you replace it? We have nothing. No beds, couches, TVs, nothing. I even thought this right here is to big for God.

We might get a dish or two but we most certainly wont get a house full of furniture right? Oh what a awesome God he is! See when we were in the shelter I happened to share my story with one of the workers that came in to help. There were hundreds of people in that shelter. Tons of families. She called me within a week of moving into our home. She said hey girl have ya'll gotten any donations for your house yet? I said no ma'am. Ok will you be home tomorrow? Yes. Ok well I'm having something delivered to you I just need you to sign for it. Ok no problem. Boy was I not ready for God to blow my mind.

When God says he will give exceedingly and abundantly he does just that. I honestly expected a donated couch. Well it was more than just a donated couch. Her brother wanted to bless someone after the hurricanes devastation and was looking for a way to give back. The truck showed up and I signed for it. When they opened the truck I dropped to my knees. It was a whole house full of furniture. I mean every room. Bunk beds for the children, a toddler bed, a full bedroom set for me etc.. I couldn't believe it! The story doesn't end there.

This woman showed up the next day with tvs, a game system, gift cards, blankets for the kids and the list goes on. God has truly sustained me. Its so hard to see Gods hand when your in the middle of the storm. When you can't see him and you can't hear him how in the world can you trust him? God why in the world do these battles keep coming? Make it stop! At times it feels that you can barely keep your head above water. If I'm your child and you love me why am I experiencing so much pain? Because my child if I don't plant you how will you grow? See I had to be deeply planted, fertilized and watered before I could begin to grow. I am a very stubborn plant.

Empowered through Pain

In Matthew 14 God sent the wind and the waves to force Peter out of the boat.

The scripture reads "And when the disciples saw Him walking on the sea, they were troubled, saying, "It is a ghost!" And they cried out for fear.

27 But immediately Jesus spoke to them, saying, [c]"Be of good cheer! [d]It is I; do not be afraid.

"28 And Peter answered Him and said, "Lord, if it is You, command me to come to You on the water."

29 So He said, "Come." And when Peter had come down out of the boat, he walked on the water to go to Jesus.

30 But when he saw [e]that the wind was boisterous, he was afraid; and beginning to sink he cried out, saying, "Lord, save me!

"31 And immediately Jesus stretched out His hand and caught him, and said to him, "O you of little faith, why did you doubt?"

32 And when they got into the boat, the wind ceased".

SO often times God has sent the wind and the rain to force me out of the boat. I comply and step forth but then I get weary and doubt God. "God save me!" I cant see your plan. I don't understand it. How in the world can I walk on water? God I know its you shifting me but why?

All I can say is trust him! Lean not on your own understanding but in all ways acknowledge him! Every good and perfect thing works according to his will. The Lord will prepare a table for you in the presence of your enemies! I'm here to tell you your pain has a purpose. Every single battle I've faced God has shown up. He's never given me just enough, he's always gone above and beyond.

Thru the many seasons of my life, despite it all I have NEVER lacked! Do you hear me? I may not have always had what I wanted but I've always had more than what I needed. It has never been my timing. Always his. I am hear to tell you the battles don't stop. God has a purpose for you and the enemy is going to try and defeat you ever chance he gets. You have a choice- you can choose to let your pain defeat you or you can allow it to empower you.

Empowered through Pain

7 I AM's

I AM FEARFULLY AND WONDERFULLY MADE

I AM MORE THAN A CONQUERER

I AM A KINGS KID

I AM NOT DEFINED BY MY PAST

I AM COURAGEOUS

I AM CALLED AND CHOSEN

I AM VALUABLE TO GODS KINGDOM.

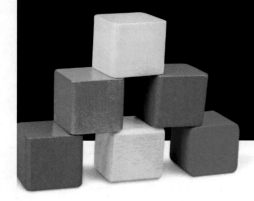

Empowered through Pain

My name is Kayleigh Keithline. I was born 8/8/88. Eight is supposed to represent new beginnings. Looking back I feel my life has been nothing but trials and new beginnings. I can honestly say I never really had a come to Jesus moment. I grew up Methodist. I remember going to church every Sunday with my grandfather and it was horrible. I have ADHD and it was so incredibly difficult to sit there and "hear the word". Traditional Methodists are not "hype" about Jesus. Don't get me wrong, I'm sure they love the Lord but it sure wasn't exciting. I don't believe I learned much during that time.

At the age of 12 I was sent to a group home that was faith based. We were required to attend church on Wednesdays and Sundays. This is the first time God became interesting to me and I wanted to know more. I became baptized and saved around this age but I was no where near living for the Lord. My heart wasn't on fire for Jesus. Through the years I continued to pursue God but I wasn't on fire. I prayed but he wasn't the center of my life. I got saved and recommitted a few more times but it never really "took off". Remember how I said earlier that your circle is important? It is very important! For years I surrounded myself with "friends" that I chose and thought I needed. I believe there is a season for everything. I thank God for each and every friendship I've had along the way but friends from the past weren't pushing me. They weren't concerned about my walk with God.

They weren't concerned about pushing me into my purpose. I cant stress enough the importance of having like minded individuals in your circle. SO fast forward the story- I continued to struggle with my relationship with God. I was expecting so much from him yet I was giving so little in return. In 2019 one of my current friends pushed me to try the SOW. I made up every excuse in the book{as I usually would} about why I couldn't go. I was already attending a church why should I try a new one? Mind you I belonged to a church but I hardly ever went. EXCUSES! I finally agreed to go. It was a Wednesday night. In my adult life I cant remember going to church on a Wednesday. Walking through the doors I immediately felt the presence of God.

An experience I've never had before. The pastor is amazing. He lights a fire in me that I've never experienced before. Since beginning the church I've attended every Wednesday and every Sunday. I did miss one week because I was sick. Suddenly I was on fire for God and it felt amazing. It was and is the pastor of the church, the atmosphere of the church, the members and my circle that is keeping my fire lit. I have a passion to serve God and his people. I want to get it right and walk in exactly who he has called me to be.

Empowered through Pain

From Pain to Purpose

I went from angry to understanding that I was anointed

I went from broken to being so Brave!I went from careless to courageous.

I went from rejected to restored

I went from irrational to intentionalI went from pain to promotion.

Promotion in everything God has in store for me.

I went from fear to first.

I was always afraid because I was never some ones first pick.

Now I know that God picked me first

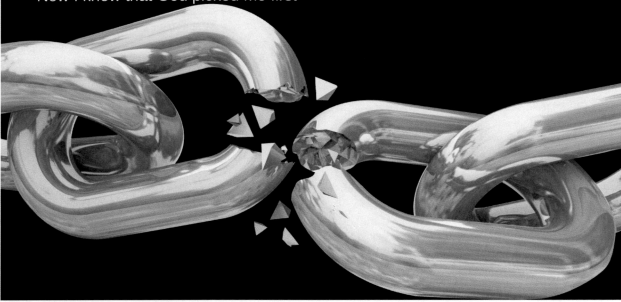

Empowered through Pain

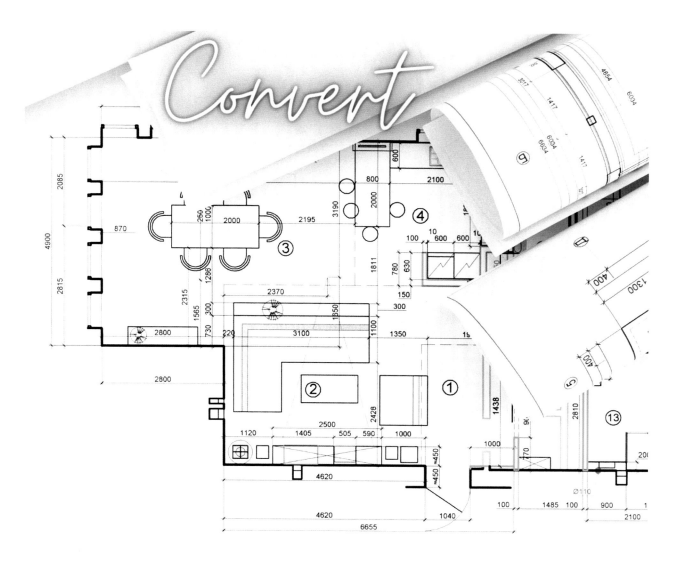

Today I am evolving into the person God has called me to be. I am no longer allowing my past to define or control me. I realize my past has purpose. Today I walk boldly and confidently in exactly who God has called me to be.

1   2   3   4

You control your destiny. Life is full of decisions. Some that are very difficult and challenge us to our core. Realistically there have been times that I've questioned God. I've had pitty parties and I've been down right angry with God. What is most important is the decisions you make and your relationship with your father. Stop making excuses and get to work. Allow God to guide you. He will see you through. My hope is that in sharing part of my story it will empower you in some way to find your purpose.

Father God your awesome! I thank you for the amazing woman/man of God that is reading these words. Pray this prayer with me:Lord I thank you for the specific calling you have over my life.

I am thankful you chose me. You knew me before I was formed in my mothers womb. Lord I'm not perfect but I'm your child. I'm a kings kid. I am more than a conqueror. I am destined for greatness.

I will walk boldly and confidently in exactly who you have called me to be. Lord I trust you. Its hard. Sometimes I cant see you. I don't understand your plan. But Father I give you the wheel.

Father God help me to understand that I am not defined by my past mistakes. My past is real but it is no longer who I am. Lord help me to become empowered through the pain I have experienced.

Your word says every good and perfect thing works according to your will. I believe your word to be true Father God.

Help me to seek you for guidance Lord. Your word says in 2nd Corinthians 12:9 But he said to me, "My grace is sufficient for you, for my power is made perfect in weakness."

Therefore I will boast all the more gladly of my weaknesses, so that the power of Christ may rest upon me. Father thank you that your grace is sufficient. Thank you that the power of Christ rests in me.

Continue to help me grow daily Father.

I ask these things in your son Jesus name-Amen.

Empowered through Pain

Chapter 9

"A Daughter of the King: From Rejection to Rejoicing"

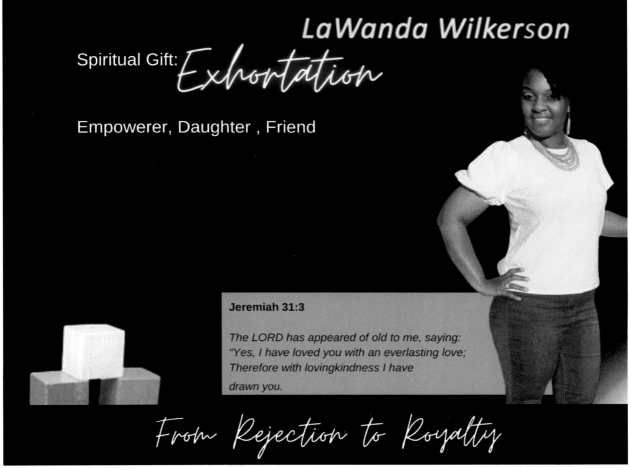

LaWanda Wilkerson

Spiritual Gift: Exhortation

Empowerer, Daughter , Friend

Jeremiah 31:3

The LORD has appeared of old to me, saying: "Yes, I have loved you with an everlasting love; Therefore with lovingkindness I have drawn you.

From Rejection to Royalty

I believe I have the divine ability and strength to build up, encourage, comfort, and motivate others to action through the written or spoken word and Biblical truth. The title of my blueprint is "A Daughter of the King: From Rejection to Rejoicing".

I believe I am called to love on and empower today's youth and their families through the word of God and love of God. Having a firm conviction to help this demographic realize their individual and collective worth in the eyes of God.

I can identify with the feelings that you feel right now. Rejection and feelings of unworthiness will breed other negative cycles in your life. If left unchecked, you may find yourself with thoughts of suicide, self-hate, and feeling unloved. This negative thought pattern is a lie and goes against everything that God has declared about you in His word.

DO NOT believe the lie the enemy is speaking to you! For every lie spoken, you must replace it with truth from the word of God. Remember, Ephesians 6:12 tells us: we do not wrestle with flesh and blood, but against principalities, against powers, against the rulers of the darkness of this age, against spiritual hosts of wickedness in the heavenly places.

The enemy is after your mind. If he can get you to think the opposite of what God has said about you in His written word, then my friend, you will succumb to the tricks and schemes of the enemy. Everyday you wake up is a battle for your peace of mind. I urge you to get into the habit of guarding your heart and protecting your mind. You may ask, "How do I guard my heart and protect my mind?" I am glad you asked!

You can guard your heart and protect your mind by reading, speaking, and applying what God's word says about you. Application of the word is a must! Meditate on the word. Prayer is another tool that will help you communicate with God.

I am sharing my testimony because I want you to overcome the spirit of rejection which has come to rob you of your joy and self-worth.

From Rejection to Royalty

If you're reading this declare this out loud

7 I Am's

I am loved.....Jeremiah 31:3

I am chosen.....1 Peter 2:9

I am a daughter of the King....Isaiah 43:1

I am made new.....2 Corinthians 5:17

I am transformed.....Romans 12:2

I am powerful and not pitiful....2 Timothy 1:7

I am whole.....Luke 17:19

From Rejection to Royalty

Confess

My name is LaWanda, those close to me call me Wanda. I grew up as a child with feelings of fear and rejection. In my home, I witnessed domestic violence and alcohol abuse. I have witnessed physical and mental abuse by the hands of an individual. I had a love hate relationship towards this individual which caused me great emotional stress and fear. I withheld and suppressed my emotions by burying them and covering them up, so I thought. Growing up, I always sensed an overwhelming feeling of fear and rejection. It was as if a shadow of both followed me, even in my dreams.

I believe part of this shadowing was due to an unsuccessful attempt to abort me. At various times in my life, the spirit of rejection caused me to want to fit in, even at the expense of making decisions that I knew were going to cost me in the long run. I sought for love and feelings of worth from relationships and others because I did not love myself.

At one point in highschool, I was suicidal. I did not see any value or self-worth in LaWanda. I just wanted to "stop breathing". I wanted the pain and feelings of rejection to go away. Thank God for his grace and mercy! I spoke those words in class and was sent to see a school counselor. The love, encouragement, and concern from the counselor allowed me to feel her compassion towards me. I witnessed the love of God in action. I walked away that day feeling a little better about myself. Seeking validation from others is one of the worst things you can do to yourself. This form of abuse gives others permission to validate your worthiness. You replace your true value of your true self in the hands of others. It's as if to say, today I'm happy and I feel valuable because "I feel like they like me" or "I was included". I gave permission to those that did not love themselves to place earthly versions of worth upon me. I want you to know that your life is valuable.

God has a purpose and plan for your life! You were born and destined for purpose!! He loves you and has called you by name, you are his!! If you ever feel like you don't belong, just remember that God loves you with an everlasting love and you belong to God! God has not made any mistakes concerning you. I am a high school teacher and I seek ways to encourage my students to love and believe in themselves. I seek to show them love in my classroom, something they may not experience at home. My yes to God, is allowing me to help others in ways that God predestined me to!! You have a God given assignment in your life. I found purpose in my pain. I went from:

From Rejection to Royalty

From Pain to Purpose

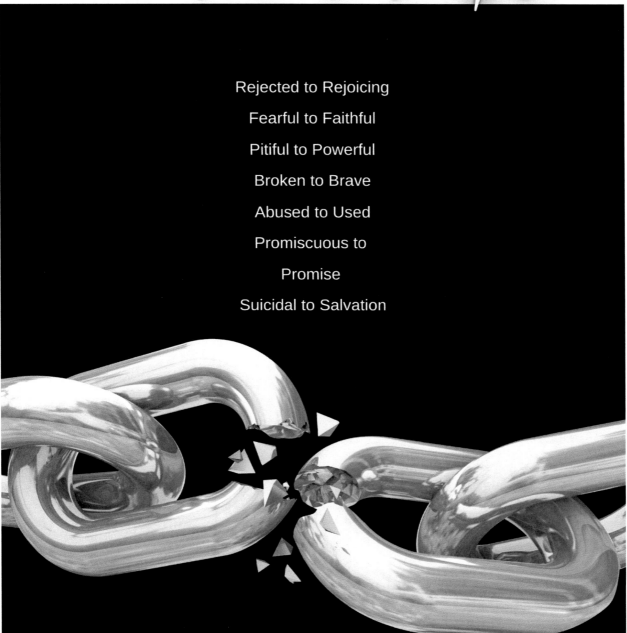

Rejected to Rejoicing

Fearful to Faithful

Pitiful to Powerful

Broken to Brave

Abused to Used

Promiscuous to
Promise

Suicidal to Salvation

From Rejection to Royalty

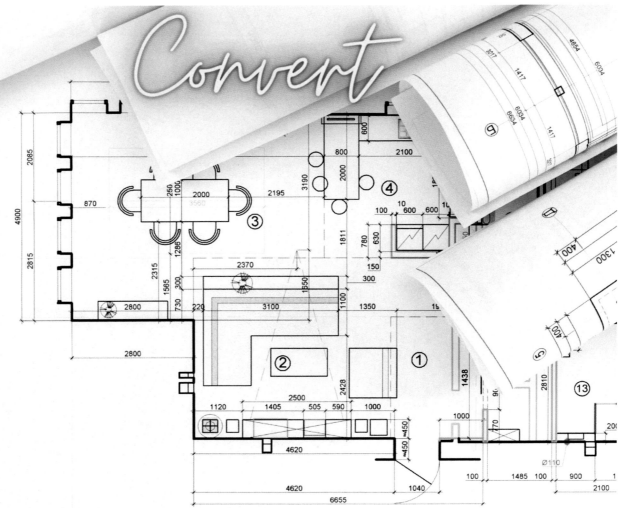

Today I am confident! Today I am brave! Today I am powerful!! And you could be too!I want you to look past the moment you are in right now, past the feelings of unworthiness and rejection, past the hurt of abuse and trauma, past the fear of who you think you are or where you think you should be in life. Yield all of those feelings and emotions to God. You may kneel, scream, throw your hand up, jump up and down, quietly meditate; whatever you have to do to get your release..do it! As you begin to release, you will feel the presence of God filling you with every good thing that you were void of. Father, I yield all hurt, abuse, and trauma to you right now in the name of Jesus!

1   2   3   4

Father,

I receive healing in every area right now.

Lord, your word says you heal the brokenhearted and binds up their wounds. Thank you for my healing. I believe that my heart and emotions are being healed right now in the name of Jesus! I denounce a spirit of rejection over my life.

I receive the spirit of rejoicing now in the name of Jesus. I forgive those who have hurt me and I forgive myself for those I have hurt. Father, I receive a new mind and a new way of thinking. I will allow my mind to be transformed by your word.

God you have not given me a spirit of fear but of power, love, and sound mind. I am made whole!! I will prosper and be in good health even as my soul prospers.

Lord, I receive the Spirit of Adoption and your everlasting and endless love you have for me.

I am loved by God and I am worthy of His inheritance!!

From Rejection to Royalty

Chapter 10

"Temple Rebuilder"

Erica Derr

Spiritual Gift: *Discernment*

Overcomer, Intercessor , Warrior,

Sister Friend

Psalms 46: 5

God is within her, she will not fall;

God will help her at break of day.

Temple Rebuilder

I believe I am called to be a Temple Rebuilder for the kingdom , a life coach in a sense, but I would tackle the whole body inwardly and outwardly (mind, body, and soul). Helping you to heal from within through God's love and understanding who you are in Christ, so you can be confident and bold and walk into your purpose that God has set for you.

"Do you not know that your body is a temple of the Holy Spirit, who is in you, whom you have received from God? You are not your own; you were bought at a price, **Therefore honor God with your body." 1 Corinthian 6:19-20 (NIV)**

I am sharing with you because I want to show you how far God has brought me and kept me my whole life! I want to encourage you that it truly does not matter what you have done, where you came from, what race you are, whatever your background may be, whatever sins you have committed, whatever dark place you are in and think it's impossible to get out. I am living proof, you're talking to a fornicator, 4 children out of wedlock to three different men, in the streets, partying with who I thought was the best, getting drunk and driving more times than I can count, homeless, domestic violence, abuse after abuse, health issues, weight problems, financial problems, you name it, whatever it is, nothing is impossible for our God. He is our miracle worker, way maker, promise keeper, light in our darkness (yes that's one of my favorite worship songs) but He is and He needs you and your story to help bring more souls to His kingdom. You are so important in God's eyes, read (Matthew 6:25)(Matthew 10:30)(Phillipians 4:13)(Proverbs 27:17), those are just a small example of who you are in God's eyes.

Once you start digging in the word you will see just how valuable you are!

Temple Rebuilder

If you're reading this declare this out loud

7 I AM's

I am a daughter/son of a king, the Alpha and Omega, the miracle worker.

I am fearfully and wonderfully made, for he is within me, I will not fall, he knows every hair on my head, he has a plan to prosper me and not harm me.

I am a victor, for the battle is already won, I am made in his image.

I am a conqueror, I will no longer be defeated.

I am very important in God's eyes, he needs me for his kingdom.

I am more precious than rubies, I am virtuous, I am clothed with strength and dignity. I laugh without fear of the future.

I am called, I do have a purpose, I am to walk in confidence in the Lord, and spread the love of Christ to anyone I come in contact with.

Temple Rebuilder

My name is Erica and this is my story. Growing up I dealt with my dad being an alcoholic battling with the abuse from his childhood, while my mom was always working. My sister and I were exposed to a lot of different things at a young age, that we really should not have been, including possible sexual abuse with me, and definetely with my sister and several different men. Because of these dramatic events we started seeing a therapist early on in life. Shortly after my dad cheated on my mom he decided to change his life around.

He gave up alcohol and gave his life to the Lord, my mom followed. When I was 15 my best friend Sasha took me to her church, I got baptized, saved, and filled with the Holy Spirit. Shortly after I became pregnant with my son Malachi to a boy in the church. I was 16 and pregnant. I was still able to graduate high school and continue on to college where I ended receiving my Associate degree for Physical Fitness Specialist.

Although it took me 9yrs to get that degree I vowed to get it done. In the meantime I was living a "lukewarm" christian life. In and out of church and my relationship with God. I was making bad decisions in life. I started dating a drug dealer, taking my son back and forth to Philly, carrying drugs in my vehicle, going into crack houses, cooking, bagging it, putting my son in danger. I got pregnant by him. I lost that baby and had to get a D+C, shortly after I finally left him. I got with yet another drug dealer and ended up pregnant with my son Micah. This relationship put me through it as well especially with his cheating. I left him and a few years later decided I needed a big change.

I left the comfort of my home state and moved to North Carolina with my boys. I thought it would be a new beginning for us and I could focus more on God, but I failed miserably. I continued choosing men that were not good for me. I left the "street" men alone thinking I'm making a better choice by them being "family oriented" men, having a legit job, believing in God, etc..but I still dealt with abuse after abuse. At one point I turned away from God, due to all these failed worldly relationships.

I was at a point in my life where I was so angry, hurt, bitter and defeated. I then met my daughters Kemena and Zoya's dad. He was funny, he was a great father, overall a good man to others, but he did not know how to love correctly, he did not have God in his life, and he hurt me in a whole other way. It was constant lying, cheating, belittling me, and we 4 were just plain and simple unequally yoked.

Temple Rebuilder

I was far from perfect in these relationships, but I basically was searching for love in all the wrong places. I left him, and 2yrs later I meant who I thought was the man of my dreams, he treated me better than any man I've ever been with, but he ended up almost killing me twice.

That a physically abusive relationship was my rock bottom! I ended up losing everything, went into shelter, temporary housing then to my current home. God and my children were my motivation to keep going.

I had to rebuild from the bottom. I thank God for that turning point in my life. I still struggled for the last couple years with dating, and finding myself in God. I started attending a different church, Sanctuary of Wilmington (S.O.W) and my whole life changed.

I had to find me and finally submit to God, become a God chaser and change my surroundings, people, places and things.

Through that change I've now met the love of my life, my fiance Mr. Christopher Champion and we are working on becoming a strong kingdom team to win souls for the Lord and be a light no matter where we go. I thank God for all my trials and tribulations, they made me who I am today.

I finally see what God has seen in me my whole life, now I'm unstoppable, the fire has been reignited.

Temple Rebuilder

From Pain to Purpose

Abused to being used for the kingdom

Broken to healed

Having fear to having faith

Fornacator to educator

Denied to assigned

Feeling worthless to knowing my worth

Having a worldly man to a Godly man

Drinking plain water to living water

Defeated to more than a conqueror

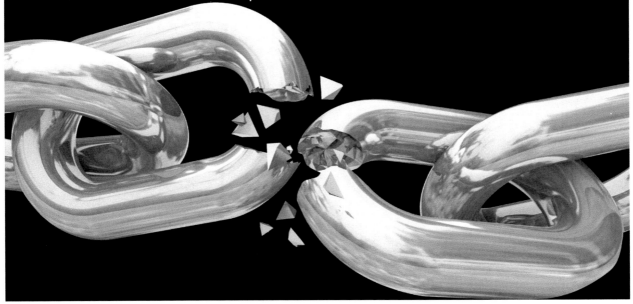

Temple Rebuilder

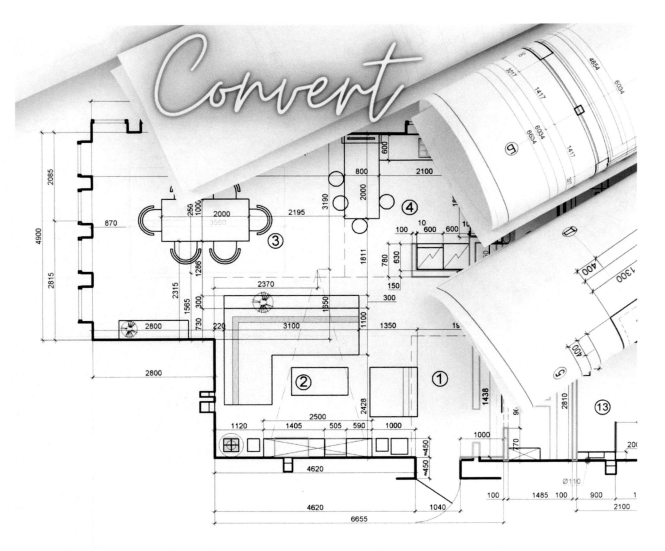

Convert

Today I am finally seeing myself through God's eyes. Healing hearts of broken, rebuilding the temple from the ground up (mentally, physically, emotionally, spiritually). Reigniting that fire from within. Assisting God here on earth with molding, shaping, changing and guiding his people, for an army is rising! I am a discerner, exhorter, pastor/shepherd, teacher, evangelist just to name a few of my God given gifts.

① ② ③ ④

I am a kingdom builder on a mission to be as Christ-like as possible and be a light in a world full of darkness. I will win millions. I will help rebuild temples so they can pour into others and help them build their God given master plans. You can be all this and more if you just give God a chance. He will not disappoint you. He has brought me through so many trials and tribulations I would be lost without him. "As iron sharpens iron, so one man sharpens another." Proverbs 27: 17 (NIV) Don't just take my word word for it, pray for yourself, speak it out loud until you believe it, do a vision board, place post-it all over, find who you are to God in the word, and yell it until you believe it!

"Everything is possible for him who believes." Mark 9:23 (NIV)

Just like my pain pushed me into purpose yours can too. We can impact others together, by being leaders instead of followers, taking action, not just talking. Helping to restore, heal, free, value, motivate, pray with, forgive, reach, unite, build, encourage, protect, make whole, win, teach, shepherd, strengthen, believe, empower, love, show kindness, mercy, favor, be an example, always speak life, listen, understand, be a light, Christlike, never give up, evolve, help change one person at a time, give God all the glory, always be thankful, walking our purpose, not be silent any longer, rebuild temples for the kingdom, and smile no matter what...because Jesus loves you!

"Come, follow me," Jesus said, "and I will make you fishers of men."
Matthew 4:19 (NIV) 6

Say this prayer with me if you feel led, and say it out loud boldly...

Lord I just want to thank you, thank you for waking me up today, thank you for your constant forgiveness. Thank you Lord for this miracle day, and giving me another chance to get it right. Thank you Lord for your healing, kindness, mercy, favor, patience, endurance, grace, and love. Lord, I ask that you continue to cover me and everyone connected to me. Help me not to lean on my own understanding and know that you only have plans to prosper me, no harm me.

Lord help me to trust you, to mold me, shape me, and change me. Show me what I need to do, and what I need to fix in me. Your will be done, not mines. Help me to use my pain for purpose , to draw me even closer to you.

Give me the wisdom I need to make Godly moves. Place a desire in me to be the God chaser I was made to be.

In Jesus name I pray. Amen!

Some worship songs that have helped me along the way. They set the atmosphere, and help me to get in the spirit.

● *Way Maker by Sinach* ● *You're Bigger by Jekalyn Carr* ● *This Is A Move by Tasha Cobbs* ● *Open My Heart by Yolanda Adams* ● *You Still Love Me by Koryn Hawthorne* ● *Let Go by DeWayne Woods*

Temple Rebuilder

Chapter I I

A divine plan out: My Exodus

Shaniqua Marshall

Spiritual Gift: *Administration*

Resilient, Leader, Service Woman, Mother, Spiritual Warrior, Teacher, Problem Solver, Patient, Determined

Psalms 46: 5

God is within her, she will not fall; God will help her at break of day.

A Divine Plan Out My Exodus

Let me first introduce myself as Shaniqua Ebony Marshall. I am a single mother of three beautiful daughters. I currently have a career as a law enforcement officer. My personality can be described as an introvert.

That being said, It is still is very challenging for me to open my personal life to others. I come from a generation of, "what happens in our house stays in our house." The fear of judgement made it difficult for me to disclose the most sensitive and traumatic incidents in my life.

I decided after redesigning my blueprint that it was very important to share my testimony, in this season. Through exposing my divine way out of bad situations, I pray this would allow you as a reader to make the decision to do the same. If you are in a traumatic place in your life or there is trauma that you have not allowed yourself to heal from, the time is now. You deserve to give yourself the best life possible.

You deserve to have Joy and sincerely feel free. Making the decision that my daughters and I deserve freedom and healing was the best thing that I could have done. We deserve the blessings God has created for us to have out of this life. Denyja', Shanice, Brooklynn, and myself deserves to live our best life.

Creating personal declarations has been a huge part of overcoming past hurt and pains in my life. The declarations have allowed me to speak over my life and make room for the words to enter the atmosphere. These are some of my personal declarations that I have learned to say every day out loud..

A Divine Plan Out - My Exodus

If you're reading this declare this out loud

7 I AM's

I am a problem solver in every area of my life.

I am surrounded by prestigious people that uplift me and chooses to be in my corner.

I am bold and fearless with any challenge I face in my life.

I am persistent in opening my businesses and completing college.

I am determined to gain wisdom and continue to grow in Christ.

I am an affluent woman to my family, community, and the body of Christ

I am healed mentally, physically, and emotionally in every area of my life.

This is declared in the name of the Father, Son, and The Holy Spirit. Amen.

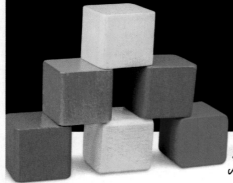

A Divine plan out My Exodus

My Place of Egypt:

Place yourself in a dark room eight months pregnant, deciding if you should just end it all. Thinking to yourself this world is so messed up, why should I allow another child in this world to be mistreated. As you stand there with the type of support where a lot of people who knows your name but chooses to not hear your cry for help. You hear a small voice inside of your head again say, "Just end it no one will miss you anyway. Besides you're a failure, your pregnant and single again. You are fat, ugly, overlooked, and you have no friends.

Where is everyone that you said had your back now? Besides your older girls will have more financially with you not here." As you sit on the side of the bed of what started as a minute, turned into hours. Another day of locking yourself from the world and contemplating, is this the day I will have the courage to just end the pain once and for all?

This was the point in my life that I realized that I have hit rock bottom. Suicidal thoughts and Depression was not something that I would have ever dreamed of experiencing in my thirties.

Everyone knew me as a strong person who loved to encourage and stand in the gap for others. Smiling was makeup, at this point in my life, it concealed so much pain and hurt. Being pregnant forced me to deal with a lot of traumatic incidents from my past that I concealed.

My Exodus

"Stop asking God what is my talent. Begin asking him what am I anointed to do. It takes anointing to shake the world," stated Sarah Jakes Roberts. After hearing this service, I pleaded and cried out for God to send me a divine answer to my questions. What am I anointed to do? What is my purpose on this earth? I honestly prayed in anger and frustration. God choose talk to me in a dream. This was my first introduction to Redesigning my Blue Print. He warned me about distractions that were preventing me from going to another level spiritually.

God specifically placed Pastor Khalilah Olokunola in the dream on the level that he has called me to. God gave me specific instructions for my season of Exodus, through this dream. In the dream, there was also a crowd that gave me instructions to come back down from the level God anointed me to be on. In this crowd was familiar faces from my circle and cloud of witnesses. They coached me to remain on the level they were on, because it made them comfortable. This was my confirmation to complete the Master Class of Redesigning My Blueprint taught by Pastor Kahalilah Olokunola. **This was the beginning of the Exodus. God revealed, it was time to let go of the old Shaniqua Marshall.**

A Divine Plan Out - My Exodus

From Pain to Purpose

After redesigning my blue print, I learned to take my pain and use them to learn my purpose.

The pain that I experienced in my life are abortion, church hurt, infidelity, domestic abuse, outcast, molestation, abandonment, homelessness, broken relationships, and death of loved ones. After seeing this pain written down on paper I couldn't help but ask myself, how can this embarrassing trauma possible contribute to my purpose? Through focus on positive language and visualizing my goals the answer was revealed.

Shaniqua went from self-condemnation to freedom
Shaniqua went from Unchurched to Called to purpose
Shaniqua went from Betrayed to Forgiveness and faithful
Shaniqua went from Sexual Aversion to Intimacy with Christ
Shaniqua went from Fatherless to abundance with Abba
Shaniqua went from homelessness to many Mansions
Shaniqua went from Mishandled/ Displaced to welcomed in the Body of ChristWhen God reveals revelation to you or use his anointed leaders to pour into your life, be obedient and write it down. It revealed how God has brought me from, pain to purpose.

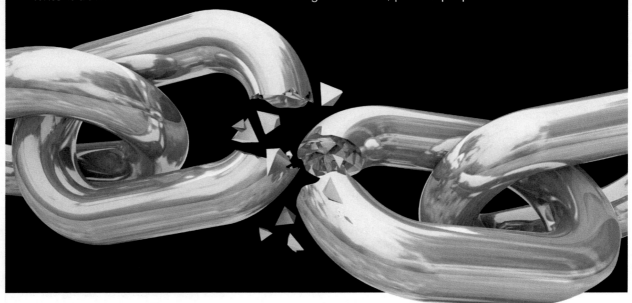

A Divine Plan Out - My Exodus

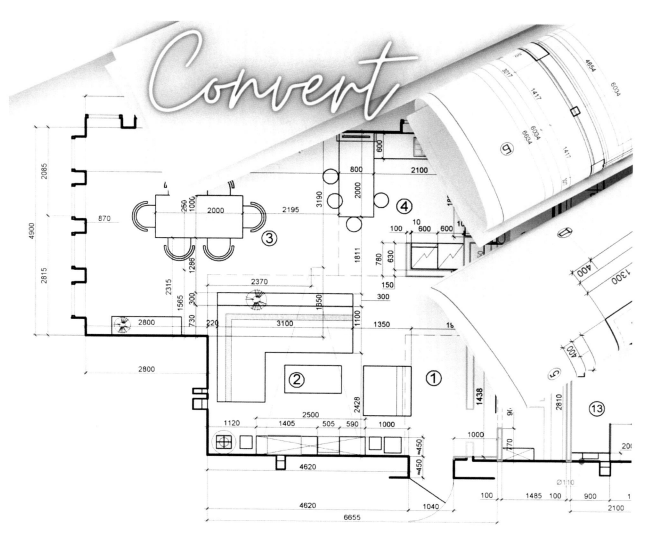

Today I am working on the ministries and assignments that I have recently discovered inside of myself. Because God has brought me out of a very dark places in my life, it is my desire to help someone else. Some of the ministries that I am working to developing will help people that went through abortion, encourage the unchurched, help those that are dealing with domestic violence, intercede against depression, homeless, woman's ministry, and woman dealing with unplanned pregnancy.

The things that I have encountered has developed a passion inside of me to help God's children with their coming out season. My focused has shifted from the experiences that caused me stress to using them to reach the purpose on my life. The pain that I experienced throughout my life, awarded me access to the places that the Lord has anointed me to go. My pain gave me the credibility and experience to operate in these ministries.

The beauty of changing your language and building your confidence plays a huge part in the transition of coming out of the old you.

These are some example the help you begin the process of getting rid of the old you.
Bold versus Fearful: Confidence that what I have to say or do is true and right in the sight of God, (Acts 4:29)
Creativity versus Underachievement: Approaching a need, a task, an idea from a new perspective, (Romans 12:2)
Availability versus Self-Centeredness: Making my own schedule and priorities secondary to the wishes of those I am serving, (Philippians 2: 20-21)

I, Shaniqua Marshall have addressed my past pain that I was harboring and the new pain that I have experienced. They have positioned and qualified me for ministry and warfare. Through reading A Divine Way Out: My Exodus it is my prayers that you will experience the presence of God in your life on a higher level.

Do not ignore your gifts for fear of drawing to much attention, church hurt, accountability, leaving your comfort zone, loosing friends, rejection, past failure, life trauma, and lack of understanding. I pray that you not only decided to get out of your trauma but you allow yourself to create a blueprint toward your ministry. The best part of your coming out season is being able to minister and encourage others.

Dear Heavenly Father, Abba I would like to first thank you for the life of your child that is currently reading this. God I thank you for their decision to invest in this guide as a reference to build a relationship with you Christ. Because of their obedience and seeds they have sown into this ministry, may they receive overflow. God I pray their life reaches the stability that you designed for them to experience.

May they have healing in their body, spirit, and heart. If they are dealing with any offenses that is holding them back, may they receive an anointing that allows them to forgive and rebuild. Lord, I feel that someone reading is having trouble forgiving themselves. As they cry at night in the bed with fear and thoughts of being alone, allow them feel your presence Lord. Allow them to know that they will never be alone for You will forever be with them. God I speak ministries that you have placed inside of them begin the process of birthing. Businesses will open, hearts will be healed, and relationship will be rebuild in the name of Jesus. If there is anyone that is in their life to distract or destroy the fire of the Holy Spirit that you have placed inside of the reader, allow them to be removed from their life. This is a new season of access and we declare this reader will receive everything that God intended for them to receive. May this beautiful spirit of God Redesign their Blue print and receive their moment of Exodus.

In the name of the Father, Son, and Holy Spirit-Amen. God Bless you and remember the importance of writing down your divine way out. **This is your Exodus.**

A Divine Plan Out - My Exodus

Chapter 12

I am Chosen, You are Chosen

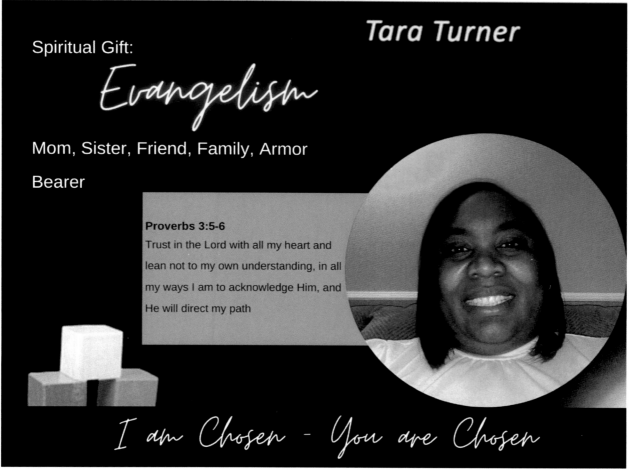

Tara Turner

Spiritual Gift:

Evangelism

Mom, Sister, Friend, Family, Armor Bearer

Proverbs 3:5-6

Trust in the Lord with all my heart and lean not to my own understanding, in all my ways I am to acknowledge Him, and He will direct my path

I am Chosen - You are Chosen

Connect

My name is Tara Turner and I have been blessed with the opportunity to be a part of Pastor Khalilah Olokunola ReDesigning the Blueprint Master Class back in July 2020. Within this class I learned that everything that I have been through in my life is the very foundation of my testimony which is my blueprint. I learned how to use the pain that I encountered for God's purpose over my life & from the Spiritual Gifts test we took, I learned that my strongest and top gift is Evangelism.

Defined from the Oxford Languages dictionary, the word Evangelism means

"1. The spreading of the Christian gospel by public preaching or personal witness.

2. Zealous advocacy of a cause. This was my top gift from the test; however, I felt that my second top gift, Exhortation, works right along with Evangelism.

Exhortation defined by the same dictionary above means "an address or communication emphatically urging someone to do something."I believe this test is spot on because I do not hesitate to speak about the goodness of the Lord and all he has done for family, friends and me and within His Word.

I have seen where my family & I had no food to eat and money was so low that I couldn't even buy groceries. I held fast in knowing that I am a child of the Most High God and that I am to trust in the Lord with all my heart and lean not to my own understanding, in all my ways I am to acknowledge Him, and He will direct my path (Proverbs 3:5-6).

I went to the Lord in prayer after looking in the refrigerator and freezer, and I prayed to Lord Jesus how and what I will feed my family. I bet it was not even 10 minutes after I prayed, my cousin Michael stopped by my house out of nowhere and dropped off 3 boxes filled with food that would last my family for weeks until I was paid again. BUT GOD! Then, I heard the Lord speak to me and He said, "I told you in my Word (The Bible) that never shall the righteous be forsaken nor the seed begging for bread." All I could do was breakdown into tears, and begin to praise Him.

I am Chosen - You are Chosen

My beloved brothers and sisters please know that our Heavenly Father loves you oh so much that He came down in the flesh in the form of the Son named Jesus to be a living sacrifice for the entire world to have an opportunity to be saved and gain eternal life.

Before His crucifixion, Jesus told His disciples that He would leave us with the Comforter, which is our Heavenly Father's Holy Spirit. His Holy Spirit was left here for us to be able to be in His Presence while still being here in the World, and to let us know that we are never alone. Here is where you see the Trinity: God the Father, God the Son and God the Holy Spirit are one. Here's an example, let's look at water. If you leave water in its original state it's a liquid, but if you place water at a freezing temperature; it becomes solid, however, if you place water in a boiling hot temperature; it becomes a vapor. A solid, a liquid and a vapor all came from one thing that is water. The three are one.

Understand this my brothers and sisters, Tara has done her share of dirt before saying yes to Jesus and even after my yes to Jesus. I have lied. I have stolen. I have taken life multiple times. I have fallen short of God's Glory numerous times. I have failed tests and trials that He has placed before me repeatedly. I have disrespected my parents, and after being saved, I have got mad at Him for not speaking to me when I wanted and needed Him to, and allow the plate of the last supper to pass me by. But God is like no other father and when He did finally speak to me, He told me the following: 1. I am Forgiven. I am Loved. I am fearfully and wonderfully made. I am a child of a Royal Priesthood. I am the Head and not the tail. I am the daughter of a King. I am Redeemed.My beloved brothers and sisters, I am here to let you know that you too are all of the above, and there is nothing that you can do nor say that our Heavenly Father cannot bring you out of. All you have to do is just what His Holy Word, The Bible says to do in Romans 10:9-10 and in Proverbs 3:5-6 (This one is my favorite!). If you have confessed Jesus as your Lord and Savior, and you believe in your heart He has been raised from the dead; you are saved. Your belief in your heart and the confession from your mouth sealed your salvation to Jesus. Will you have mishaps, absolutely! However, they will be part of your own blueprint and foundation, which is your testimony.Let me share this with you beloved, just a few months ago, I started to receive messages from the Lord like a sermon almost. In fact, in some cases it actually was a sermon for someone that needed to receive a Word from the Lord through my testimony. Check this out; I spoke earlier on how I took life, which translate in having an abortion, more than once. For years, I carried that guilt over me because I felt that God would not dare forgive me because for one I knew what I was doing, and for two this was a commandment from God that Thou shall not kill. I repented every time and asked for His forgiveness, but the guilt was still there.

I am Chosen - You are Chosen

I remember receiving an email with a biblical message from my best friend's mother and the Lord led to call her. I began explaining to her what I was feeling and her response was priceless. She said,

"Tara, the Lord has already forgiven you when you went to Him and repented and asked for His forgiveness. He at that very moment took what you were asking and threw it into the Sea of Forgetfulness. Sweetie, the problem now is that you are allowing the enemy to keep you from forgiving yourself.

Tara you have to forgive yourself too sweetheart because Jesus has forgave you!" I broke down into tears, and started to thank and praise God. I said aloud that I forgive myself and that the enemy can no longer use this over me, in Jesus name, Amen!

When I tell you that weight that I was carrying and holding onto the Lord Jesus stepped in and took it all

I am Chosen - You are Chosen

7 I AM's

I am a sinner in need of a Savior and I have found salvation in the Lord Jesus.
I am chosen by the Most High God to fulfill His purpose over my life and to live by
His Will, which is His Word, every single day of my life.

I am Chosen. Right now, I am redesigning myself for all the Gifts, Purpose, Will
and Calling from my Heavenly Father and Lord and Savior over my life.

I am called to speak and reach out to all of God's people no matter where their
walk is at this present time and to encourage them, and let them know that there
is no sin that the Lord Jesus will not forgive according to His Holy Word.

I will sustain myself by always going to God in prayer and waiting for a reply
along with reading His Word daily and meditating on it.

I am Chosen – You are Chosen

After going through the ReDesigning the Blueprint Masterclass, I am so much more confident in walking in my Gifts and my Purpose from God, and understand that my testimony is my story and foundation to achieve everything the Lord has in store for me.

I no longer feel that I am less than or unworthy to be used by my Heavenly Father, and be able to identify when the enemy or myself tries to deter me from my Calling and God's Purpose.My prayer for you is that you understand that you too are chosen, and that the Lord is always there with His arms open wide to receive you, just as He did me.

Pray this prayer with me: Lord Jesus, I come before you to first thank you for sacrificing yourself for me and those of this world.

Forgive me Lord for I am a sinner in need of a Savior. I believe in my heart and have confessed with my mouth that You Lord Jesus are raised from the dead. I believe that you have full authority over this world and Heaven above. Lord Jesus You have conquered death, Hell and the grave by Your Resurrection.

Save me O Lord and show me Thy Will and Thy Purpose that You bestowed over me. I declare and decree that on this day I stand on the solid rock which is Your Holy Word.

I bind myself to every Yes and Amen, as well as, every promise that You speak of in Your Word.

You are the same; God the Father, God the Son and God the Holy Spirit and the three are one. Hear me O Lord for this is my prayer to Thee, in Jesus name I pray, Amen.

I am Chosen - You are Chosen

From Uncomfortable to Confident

I am Chosen - You are Chosen

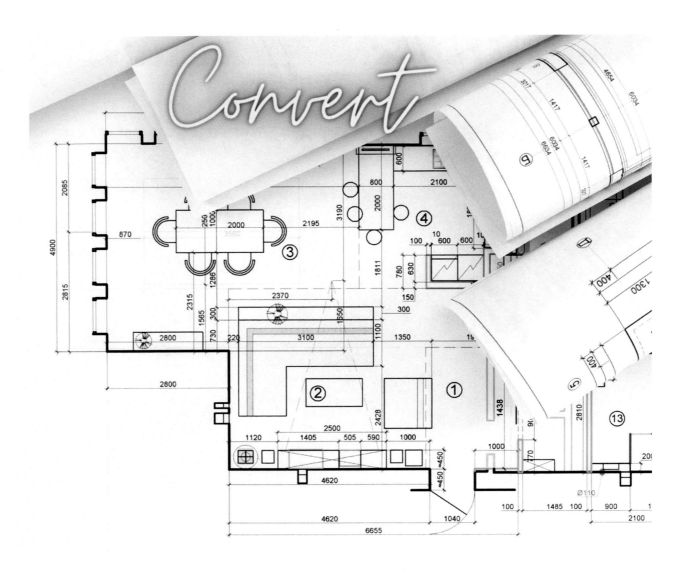

Now get your praises on my beloved brothers and sisters, and know that you are all loved by the Most High God, your Lord and Savior Jesus the Christ and by me! God bless you all!

① ② ③ ④

In Closing

We hope that this book blessed you

Are you shaken, stirred and stretched to soar so that you can make Kingdom Impact?
It's in you , it's always been there ! All you needed was someone to pull, push and provoke you to position yourself in a posture of purpose so that God can use you !

It's your time , season and the reason is never about you but the nations you are called to impact .

In closing , ask yourself what does my blueprint look like ?
How can what I went through impact someone who is going through ?
How can I use my testimony as a tool to increase faith, fortitude and fight in the lives of others.
The bible tells us in revelations 12:11
And they overcame him by the blood of the Lamb and by the word of their testimony, and they did not love their lives to the death
That means that there are 3 ways that we overcome trials. 3 ways that we overcome tribulations , 3 ways that we overcome the accuser of the brethren .
Those ways are :

- **The blood of the Lamb.**
- **The word of our testimony. (Should I repeat this)**
- **Loving not our life to the death.**
-

Ask yourself today, what are you willing to release , render & then rave about out loud so that you can rally the remnant and they can rise in God .

Precious | Naomi | PKO | Sonora| Olivia|
Tara | Erica Kayleigh | LaWanda | Christie
| Carlette | Kayleigh

The Breakthrough BLueprint

Blueprint Notes

COURAGEOUSLY COMMISSIONED

REIGNING IN ROYALTY

BRIGHT WOMEN

I AM A CHILD OF GOD

TERMS OF SERVICE

PRESSING FORWARD WITH GRACE

EMPOWERMENT THROUGH PAIN: A DAUGHTER OF THE KING

FROM REJECTION TO REJOICING

TEMPLE REBUILDER

A DIVINE PLAN OUT: MY EXIDUC

I AM A CHILD OF GOD

I AM CHOSEN * YOU ARE CHOSEN

PRESSING FORWARD WITH GRACE

EMPOWERMENT THROUGH PAIN

Made in the USA
Monee, IL
11 May 2021